ACHIEVING THE IMPOSSIBLE:
INTIMATE MARRIAGE

ACHIEVING THE IMPOSSIBLE:
INTIMATE MARRIAGE

Charles M. Sell
FOREWORD BY HOWARD HENDRICKS

MULTNOMAH · PRESS

Portland, Oregon 97266

Cover design and illustration: Paul Lewis

ACHIEVING THE IMPOSSIBLE—INTIMATE MARRIAGE
© 1982 by Multnomah Press
Portland, Oregon 97266

First Printing 1982

Library of Congress Cataloging in Publication Data

Sell, Charles M., 1933-
    Achieving the impossible—intimate marriage.

    Bibliography: p.
    Includes index.
    1. Marriage—Religious aspects—Christianity.
I. Title.
BV835.S44   248.4   82-7854
ISBN 0-930014-88-X (pbk.)   AACR2

FOREWORD

Timmy, a preschooler, brought his friend into the house to meet his mother. "Mommy, this is Marcie; she's going to be my first wife."

We smile; that's cartoon copy. But underneath we grimace. Our world is beginning to believe seriously that marriage is a throwaway. We do well to reexamine this togetherness that children romanticize and many mid-lifers take for granted.

But don't we know all there is to know about matrimony? Hasn't it been examined, x-rayed, x-rated, and generally stamped as a take-it-or-leave-it item? Charles Sell has renewed the battle. "Good marriages don't happen; they are made to happen," he claims. "A good marriage comes from both judgment and adjustment."

One cannot read this book without smelling the smoke. Marriage is under attack. Is it defensible? If so, what are effective weapons? How can raw recruits make a resolute stand against the advancing divorce rate in modern America? (A rate which now exceeds the marriage rate.)

These pages announce good news. Sexual dilemma? Differences can work *for* marriage partners. "Sex is a language; you must look closely at what you are communicating."

Conflictual cul-de-sac? Like a field commander briefing his troops our author charges husbands and wives with avoiding issues— using Bible verses and sarcasm. He skillfully teaches confrontation for "tough and touchy feelings."

Who's boss? Headship is not a head trip, we learn. Power struggles invade kitchen and bedroom, as well as boardroom. Money and children are commodities for which we bid.

Here is one professor who speaks with a confident tongue to the concept of joining one man and one woman for life. I am proud to call him my friend and my colleague, an able—and recommendable—expositor of this crucial biblical issue.

Howard G. Hendricks

CONTENTS

INTRODUCTION

Marriage is what you make it.

Let's face it; that is really true. Even so, something inside of all of us resists this idea.

We want to believe someone or something else makes it. God, maybe. Romantic love, perhaps (since it makes the world spin, it ought to keep us whirling).

Why do we shy away from the idea that marriage is something we construct together—that its destiny is in our clasped hands?

Ideally we may expect marriage to be something that just happens. It is to be enjoyable, easy, and exciting . . . like tubing down a warm rapid river on a sunny afternoon. We are just carried along. Of course marriage is not like other things we experience. Shoveling snow is work. What we do from nine to five is work. But marriage—work? No. If it's work, it isn't marriage.

A lot of this feeling is due to the fact that we like things that just happen to us. We relish surprises that are not of our own doing. Marriage is put into the category of the inspired, exciting, and unexpected. Saying "marriage is what you make it," seems to rob marriage of the spontaneous, the serendipitous.

But is that really so? Things people make are still exciting. A piece of chocolate French silk pie doesn't just happen. Yet some of us will call it "delicious and exciting."

Suppose someone, as they stood peering with Michelangelo at the naked Sistine chapel ceiling, would have said to the inspired painter, "It's up to you; the painting will be what you make it." Would he not have replied, "Of course."

The fact that Michelangelo would indeed "make" the painting would not exclude other important things. Inspiration, inner fire, compulsion, love, and other inner forces would play a part. But essentially that ceiling was turned into a magnificent piece of art by an artist lying on his back, cramped and hurting, on the top of a high scaffold, for long, lonely hours.

And so it is with an intimate marriage. Like other works of art, it is not impossible. But it is work. This book intends to help you create your own marriage masterpiece.

It is for those who are still thinking about creating a marriage, whether their wedding is ahead of or behind them. The principles and pattern are the same for both since marriage is a lifelong creation. You never really feel you can say: "We've got it made."

Since every marriage is different, and since every marriage is the couple's own unique creation, I will not try to pour you into my mold. Rather I have attempted to get the "shape" and the working principles from Scripture. And I have tried to wed these principles with the realities of modern life. I don't believe we can have a biblical marriage. I believe we can have a contemporary marriage based on biblical principles.

A glance at this book will also tell you that it suggests a model of marriage that is relational. I don't think that the biblical pattern for marriage is primarily an institutional one. Marriage is not to be run like a small business, with an organizational chart and job descriptions being the key to success.

The guidelines in this book have been forged by my studying and teaching about marriage for more than twenty years. I have also drawn upon the rich, intimate experience with my wife, Ginger. You will see that I have not written only about the pleasant side of a relationship. Ginger and I have had sufficient struggles in our marriage as well as enough counseling with others to realize how complex marriage can be. It is my view that marital closeness will only grow in the soil of realism—where we attack our problems instead of letting them attack us.

The vital stuff of marriage is really known to those who are engaged in building a close relationship. God's plan for marriage is bound up in the word intimacy. *"They shall become one flesh,"* He said.

This book is designed to help the two of you make the most important discovery of all—each other.

We earnestly pray you'll make it.

CHAPTER ONE

BUILDING A HOUSE ON A VANILLA ICE CREAM FOUNDATION
THE PITFALLS OF ROMANTIC LOVE

A woman persuaded her sixty-year-old husband to come to me for counseling. Before the session she told me he was planning to leave her. After some opening small talk, I asked, "Why do you want to leave your wife?" His reply was quick, indicating he had given it a lot of thought. "I no longer love her." The feeling between them was gone.

His answer was simple enough and reasonable. If the pilot light goes out, the furnace won't heat. If the love is gone, it's gone. And love is to marriage what Elmer's glue is to a loveseat, isn't it? If the glue fails, the whole thing collapses, leaving two people helplessly sprawled on the carpet. Thus, when the emotion vanishes the marriage is over; terminated; finished; kaput. So if the life is gone, let's face it and call a corpse a corpse.

Though this is a very popular way of thinking about marriage, it has a serious, disturbing fault: a deficient view of love. Yes, love is the bond of matrimony. But it is not the kind of love that is implied in the statement: "I no longer love her."

That kind of love goes around with the handle "romantic love." It is fantastic to have in your marriage, but don't count on it to keep you together.

The Idealistic Nature of Romantic Love

One of the deficiencies of romantic love is its idealistic nature. The romantic sees everything through the proverbial rose-colored glasses. Romance has a way of coloring everything it touches, too. Not too unlike a drug trip, when an individual is gripped by this powerful emotion, his/her vision is dramatically distorted. An engaged couple stands on a bridge, talking late into the night about intimate things. They gaze for long hours at the water flowing beneath them, symbolizing their lives flowing together. Forever after, they declare, "That's our bridge." No, in reality, it belongs to the city.

Even adverse circumstances are colored pink and yellow by these romantic feelings. A sudden thunderstorm devastates their picnic. But, no matter. Tossing the soggy blanket with the lunch rolled inside into the car's back seat, they cheerfully drive off sopping wet. Forever after, they declare, "That's our storm."

There is little place for reality in the romantic perspective. The Bible confirms the reality of this fantastic human experience: Jacob loved Rachel so much, the book of Genesis informs us, he *"served seven years to get Rachel, but they seemed like only a few days to him because of his love for her"* (Genesis 29:20). That is love—the romantic variety. Like the drug trip, the weakness of the romantic trip shows up when the effect wears off and reality sets in.

"Dream in engagement, but in wedlock awake," said someone who had his feet on the ground. Awaking to reality after a time, we may find many things we dislike about our spouse. It's quite normal to be shocked to find he/she doesn't live up to our image. Said one woman to the divorce lawyer, "I married an ideal, I got an ordeal, and I want a new deal." In part, the ordeal is caused by the ideal.

When we are first romantically involved, we don't see the total person. Or else we actually (and unknowingly) distort what we see. Sometimes our romantic feelings make us ignore what is there; we see a fault, but we don't mind because we are so much in love. We even distort our own value system for a time. So much enraptured by love, we may not mind eating pizza with our partner, though we never really liked it before. As one man said, "Before we were married, she loved to go sailing with me and I was thrilled by the evenings at the symphony with her. But, after marriage, she got sick in the sailboat and I became nauseated at the symphony."

Romantic love must eventually give way to a more realistic

love. A long-term marriage cannot be sustained on illusion. We must eventually love a person for what he is, not for what he seems to be. One of the most beautiful statements I have ever read about love is this:

> Acceptance in marriage is the power to love someone and receive him in the very moment that we realize how far he or she falls short of our hopes. It is love between two people who see clearly that they do not measure up to one another's dreams. Acceptance is loving the real person to whom one is married. Acceptance is giving up dreams for reality.[1]

The Emotional Nature of Romantic Love

As if the idealistic feature of romantic love were not enough to disqualify it as a marriage base, there is another major weakness. Romantic love is primarily emotional. A humorous teenage definition of love says it all: "Love is a feeling that you feel when you feel you have a feeling that you never felt before."

It's not tough to prove that this is a prevailing contemporary view of love. Popular songs, movies, TV stories, and romantic novels press this concept upon us before we get out of sixth grade. Psychologist James Dobson notes the Partridge Family recording a few years ago which he says betrays a lack of understanding of real love. Dobson explains: "It said, 'I woke up in love today 'cause I went to sleep with you on my mind.' You see, love in this sense is nothing more than a frame of mind."[2] Another group, called the Doors, takes the prize for portraying this kind of love in their song entitled "Hello, I Love You; Won't You Tell Me Your Name!"

This 99.44 percent emotional content of romantic love makes it as fit a marriage foundation as vanilla ice cream would be for your house foundation. Because it is emotional, it is considered uncontrollable.

Romantic Love—A Happening

Romantic love happens. All the popular expressions about it tell us that: We fall in love. "The moment I saw her I fell." Somebody "turns us on." Love, like the hit songs say, hits us. Do you ever remember any of your single friends saying one evening, "Tonight I am going to go out and begin to love someone." No, romantic love is not something you "make happen"; it happens. It depends upon where Cupid decides to strike next.

While falling in love is a great place to fall, this idea of falling is a major fault of romantic love. When that sixty-year-old man said, "I no longer love her," I got the feeling that he was explaining, not apologizing. Love, for him, was something that happened to them long ago. Like some fuzzy cloud of cotton candy it descended upon the two of them, providing the only reason they needed to fall into the marital bed. But, he reasoned, if through the years my love evaporates like a pink melting glob of cotton candy, I have now lost the basis for my marriage. If something I couldn't help led me to marriage, it is now something I can't help that allows me to get out of it.

This notion of love can produce a helpless panic. I have had men frantically say to me that they are losing their love for their wives. "Does this mean," they question, "that I married the wrong girl?" "Will my marriage last?" Such thinking ignores that true love is something that we are in control of; it is something we must make happen. True, emotions are partially out of our control. Being as they are, they fluctuate a great deal. Sometimes the loving feeling goes out of a relationship for a day, a month, or more than a year.

But there are things we can do to keep our romance going. We can "make love." A full understanding of love includes my responsibility for causing love to be part of a relationship. The Apostle Paul commanded men to "love their wives," and women to "be husband lovers." Paul would not have commanded us to do something over which we have no control. Changing the marriage vows, as some do today, to say "as long as we love each other," reveals a harmful misunderstanding of what love and marriage are all about.

If romantic love could hold a marriage together, surely we would have outstanding examples of how this works. How many couples do you know who go to the altar without being madly, or at least mildly, in love? While these relationships don't seem to be lacking other things, their major deficiency is definitely not romantic love. Yet, two out of five of these marriages end in divorce.

And we have outstanding examples of unusual romantic ties that became untangled. Richard Burton and Elizabeth Taylor had an internationally celebrated marriage. Each possessing a Hollywood acclaimed body, they were intensely attractive to each other physically. Able to jet to any romantic spot in Europe for weeks of romantic evenings, they possessed all the money needed to bring into a reality the most expensive of romantic fantasies. They exchanged jewels worth hundreds of thousands of dollars. Yet their marriage did not last. Scores of other more recent examples, like national sex symbol Farrah Fawcett and manly Lee Majors, show us that while romantic love creates some spectacular relationships, it doesn't create secure ones.

One of the Blissful Bonds of Marriage

As much as you will want romance in your marriage, you will need to count on other features of your relationship to hold it together. Consider yourself bound together. Marriage is a blissful bondage and there are three biblical, practical, and sensible bonds of love. We will deal with the first bond in this chapter. The second and third bonds will be developed in the next chapter.

The first of these is found in Jesus' statement about marriage. Whenever He was asked about divorce, He spoke mostly about marriage. He knew that it would take more than good laws to keep people married. It would take good marriages, built on good concepts of marriage. Jesus' concept of marriage is taken from the Old Testament. In Genesis, Moses described marriage in the familiar words Jesus quoted: *"For this cause a man shall leave his father and mother, and shall cleave to his wife; and the two shall become one flesh"* (Matthew 19:5, NASB). The first "bond" to consider is the one found in the word cleave. Essentially, it means what you would expect: "to be joined to," "to cling to." The Hebrew word is used this way throughout the Old Testament. In Job 38:38, for example, it is used of two chunks of mud that cling together: *"when the dust becomes hard and the clods of earth stick together."* That phrase, I have often thought, would make an interesting title for an article on marriage: "When the Clods Stick Together."

With this meaning, the man cleaving unto his wife means he will be joined to her. There is an obvious reference to the sexual embrace when the interlocking of bodies symbolizes the connection that takes place. But the cleaving involves more than the sexual and emotional joining that takes place. The word cleave is also used when speaking of the loyalty that exists between individuals. Very often, this Hebrew word is used to describe people's clinging to God and His law during times of apostasy, when others were forsaking Him. Thus, Moses says in Deuteronomy 4:4: *"But all of you who <u>held fast</u> to the LORD your God are still alive today."*

It is quite theologically correct, then, to extend the meaning of "cleave" to include the idea of commitment. The entire Old Testament approach to marriage is based on the idea that the individual is obligated to be faithful to his or her personal marriage pledge. Love is a commitment.

The Bond of Committed Love

Your commitment to each other is the strongest possible marriage adhesive. That commitment is profoundly *personal.* It is one of the most personal pledges a person will ever make. Unlike joining an organization, you are not just giving your time, energy, and money. Marriage demands the offering of yourself. You commit your body, your private and inner secrets of self, in the most intimate union known to humans. Your commitment is not dependent upon the fickle impulses of romantic love. Your commitment is located in the human will. Therefore, your marriage depends upon your strength of character, not on the stability of your emotions. Whenever both of you have this kind of commitment, it lends a tremendous sense of security to your marriage.

Once you are sure that the other has fully pledged him or herself to the relationship, you have a solid sense of attachment that allows you to withstand the tensions and conflicts that arise in the relationship. If you fight, you are not fearful that you will soon see the last of each other. But you know that later you will make up and return to each other's arms because you are both committed to do so.

Such devotion is a remarkable human experience. A rich man was once testing his wife's loyalty. "Would you love me if I lost all my money?" he asked. "Yes, I would," she replied unhesitatingly. Testing her further, he put before her a second question: "Would you love me if I lost my hearing and became blind?" "Yes, even then," she said. "But," he now offered his final test, "would you love me if I lost my mind and became insane?" At this she paused, carefully weighing her answer. "Who could love a deaf, blind, and

Building a House on a Vanilla Ice Cream Foundation

penniless idiot?" she answered him. "But," she went on, "I'd take care of you." This lofty and personal commitment is like a psychological posturepedic mattress under the both of you.

But the commitment is more than personal. It is also *socially sanctioned.* I am often asked about this today. Some want to challenge the idea that marriage must be a legal thing. They ask: "Can't two people decide to live together and thus be married in the sight of God?" It is as if they are saying that whenever it becomes legal it is less personal. The biblical answer seems to be clearly "no." When a man "left his father and mother," he did so publically. From the earliest of Old Testament times, marriage was a social arrangement. There were laws regulating it. Two of the ten commandments speak about the legal aspect of marriage. If adultery were committed, the person was to be punished by society. Society needs to have a stake in marriage because stable marriages are necessary for a stable society. But this social pressure need not make the commitment less personal. Adding something to the commitment doesn't subtract anything.

Besides this personal and social aspect, Jesus adds a third dimension to your commitment—the *divine sanction. "What therefore God has joined together, let no man separate"* (Matthew 19:6, NASB). God, along with others, is a witness to your pledges. He created the marriage arrangement; when two people marry, it is as if He, Himself, has joined them. Because human promises have a divine sanction, Jesus added the warning: "Let man not separate." Dropping this spiritual factor possibly weakens marriage more than anything else. In a secular society, with God left out, human decisions and contracts have no eternal significance. Because of this, moderns have become what popular author John Powell calls "commitment cripples." But the Christian knows that "whatever you bind on earth will be bound in heaven."

This need not put us under undue pressure. We know from Scripture that divorce and annulments are allowed for *extreme* cases. Rather, when you both realize that "God has joined" you together, it adds a sense of permanency that you need. Granted, it forces you to a complete commitment, but it also assures you of your partner's full commitment to you. Imagine how much anxiety you are spared. Can you envision what it would be like to wake up every morning wondering if your partner will still decide to live with you?

Marriages are built on this bedrock of commitment. My wife, Ginger, once told me something that shows how the social, personal, and divine aspects of the marriage covenant combine as a foundation for marriage. In a moment of candor, after we had been together six years, she confided that she had thought seriously about leaving me. During the opening years of our marriage she really wanted out—badly. I was shocked. I never suspected things had been that bad; they weren't for me. Besides, "Who would possibly want to leave me," I thought. "But," she continued, "I didn't leave you because I don't believe in divorce, God doesn't believe in divorce, and my Aunt Vea didn't believe in divorce." This wonderful lady she had lived with during her teenage years had built into her the value of hanging tough in a relationship. And Ginger did. Today, more than twenty years later, we have something tremendous going in our marriage. It came not because we possessed instant compatibility; rather, it was because we had commitment.

Commune Occasion

Agree-Disagree.

This is a fun way for the two of you to exchange thoughts related to the ideas about marriage expressed in this chapter.

Read each statement out loud and decide whether or not you agree with it. In order for you to share your answer at the exact moment, do the following. Count to three. At the sound of three, each of you show either one finger meaning you agree or two fingers if you disagree.

Should you have different answers, you will have a good opportunity to share and understand each other better. Even if your answers are the same, you can profit from exchanging ideas about the statement.

- Most of the marriages I have seen are based upon the notion of romantic love, not commitment.
- Romantic love is primarily a feeling you can do nothing about.
- People who do not have strong romantic feelings for each other in the beginning probably do not have a basis for a long-lasting relationship.

- I know of several popular songs that express a good concept of mature love.
- I believe there is no reason whatsoever for two married people to separate for divorce.
- I would say that several types of love are involved in our relationship.

ENDNOTES

[1]Gibson Winter, *Love and Conflict,* quoted in Helen Kooiman Hosier, *The Other Side of Divorce* (New York: Hawthorn, 1975), p. 141.

[2]James Dobson, *What Wives Wish Their Husbands Knew About Women* (Wheaton, Ill.: Tyndale House Publishers, Inc., 1977), p. 89.

CHAPTER TWO

BONDING, NOT BONDAGE
WHAT WILL HOLD A MARRIAGE TOGETHER

A strange headline appeared in the column of the well-known answer lady, Ann Landers. The title was simply: "Ann Has No Answer." She explained.

> The sad incredible fact is that after 36 years of marriage, Jules and I are being divorced. As I write these words, it is as if I am referring to a letter from a reader. It seems unreal that I'm writing about my own marriage. That we are going our separate ways is one of life's ironies. How did it happen that something so good for so long didn't last forever? The lady with all the answers does not know the answer to this one. Perhaps there is a lesson here, at least there is for me. Never say, "It couldn't happen to us."[1]

Ann pushes an anxiety button hidden inside every married person. "Will it last forever?" we inwardly mutter to ourselves. None of us wants to partake of the hurt and hardship of separation we see so many people enduring.

The person married to a sincere Christian has an advantage. The Christian bases his marriage on a serious commitment. Not wanting a foundation of either sand or ice cream, the believer builds upon a rock: the teachings of Jesus Christ. This commitment is followed by a commitment to the other partner.

This is not to say, however, that sheer commitment is the only bond between two Christians. Talking about marriage as a promise may make it sound like a cold, heartless arrangement. However, marriage from the biblical perspective is more than this. After all, marriage is a love affair, not a business deal.

Marriage *is* a commitment to love. This is the first bond of love, discussed in the previous chapter. Marriage counselor Wayne Oates calls it "a responsible covenant of love." But our anxiety about the stableness of marriage ought to cause us to be very careful about how we think of love.

A biblical marriage is built upon two types of love. These are the other two bonds of a Christian marriage.

The Bond of Christ-like Love

When God commanded men to love their wives and for wives to be lovers of their husbands, He was speaking of Christ-like love. *"Husbands, love your wives, just as Christ loved the church and gave himself up for her."*

This kind of love differs from romantic love, as we have already discussed. Romantic love is idealistic; Christ-like love is realistic. God loves us even though He knows us truly and thoroughly. He loves us despite our faults and sins. Romantic love is emotional; Christ-like love is basically willful.

When the Bible says that "God so loved the world," we don't picture Him in heaven gushing all over and stumbling about in a starstruck daze. God willfully chose to love us. Christ-like love is not without emotion, of course, but it doesn't depend upon emotion. It involves a choice.

Christ-like love is also significantly different from romantic love in a way we haven't mentioned. His kind of love is sacrificial. *"He loved the church and gave himself up for her."* That is a one-way kind of action. He gave with the possibility He might not get anything in return. No conditions are attached. Often in our marriage we will be called upon to love in this way. During times of stress or sickness, one partner may be demanding more than he is supplying. It'll take some sacrificial loving to get over those tough spots.

Such high-sounding terms as "sacrificial love" may seem a bit idealistic and as hard to grasp as a handful of jello. Actually, Christ-like love is one of the most down-to-earth concepts I know of. The Apostle Paul brings it right down to the dust on our feet in his extremely practical description in chapter thirteen of First Corinthians. When you apply his words to marriage, you not only see where the rubber meets the road, you can smell it burning.

Love is *patient*. When your spouse provokes you, you hang in there. You wait it out and then handle the dispute calmly at another time. You don't rush the person into growth or change, either. Like a gardener you watch the other mature and blossom—with patience.

Love is *kind*. While patience is the lack of a nasty reaction, kindness is a positive reaction. Kindness reaches out to help even when the other doesn't seem to merit it. Ernest Hemingway advised every man to be kind to his wife when she least of all deserved it, because that was when she would need it the most. Good advice as well for women in regard to their husbands.

Love does *not envy*. There is no mental uneasiness over the other's success—no sulking because our partner is experiencing something we were denied.

Love does *not boast, is not proud*. It's tough to live with a proud person. Love doesn't say: "Don't you know who I am? I deserve better than this."

Love is *not rude*. The Greek word in this phrase is difficult to interpret. It probably does mean "love is not rude," as the NIV translates it. Too often we reserve our politeness for people outside the family. We think we have the liberty to treat harshly those who are close to us. Not so, says Paul.

Love is *not self-seeking*. While we can expect to get something out of marriage, this sacrificial attitude should dominate us.

Love is *not easily angered*. We would understand this better if it were translated "does not fly off the handle." Anger is not always wrong, but love doesn't lose control. Once when I was very angry with one of my sons, letting cutting words fling from my mouth, a small voice was saying inside of me:

"Chick, you're not loving." The voice was right. The next day, I apologized to him.

Love keeps *no record of wrongs*. Keeping score and getting even is destructive. Peter says *"love covers over a multitude of sins."* If you keep harboring ill feelings and ruminating on them, you'll produce enough emotional gas to make you suddenly explode like a broken furnace.

Love does not delight *in evil but rejoices with the truth*. Someone has said that you can tell when the honeymoon is over. "You are absolutely perfect" is exchanged for "the problem with you is." Faultfinding is a damaging activity that love avoids.

Love *bears all things* (NASB). Forbearance is the major ingredient of marriage, not perfection . . . just as forgiveness and not obedience is the major factor in our relationship to God. We put up with each other as God puts up with us. The woman had the right idea when she said: "Jack won't pick up his underwear and socks, but he is such a great husband in so many other ways, I'll put up with the clutter."

Love *always trusts*. To doubt someone is unloving. Love trusts. To say to your partner, "I believe in you," "I trust you," is one of the most supportive things you can do for them.

Love *always hopes*. Sometimes one of you will be despairing. Depression makes you see a black sky in every direction. Then your lover says, "there is hope—the future is better than you think."

Love *always perseveres*. Endurance doesn't mean we don't seek remedies for our marital problems. We may have to suggest counseling to improve or reconcile our relationship. But there are times when all we can do is endure. Here is the greatest quality of love: love endures all things. Jesus endured the cross.

Love *never fails*. This does not mean love always succeeds. It means it will always continue. It is one of the world's stable commodities. Love is at the heart of reality: *"And now these three remain: faith, hope and love. But the greatest of these is love."*

The Love You Choose to Do

To summarize this kind of love, Christ-like love, Paul is saying that love is something you choose to do. It is motion, not just emotion. You decide to be kind, patient, trustful. You determine not to be rude, selfish, envious, or proud. These features of love are basically actions. Love has a lot less to do with emotions than we sometimes realize.

Christ-like love is something I decide to do. I act toward a person in a loving way. This I can do even when I don't feel love for them. It is very possible to love someone you don't like. That is the essence of love—acting positively toward someone, even if he is your enemy.

Your own partner can sometimes be your enemy. Or at least there will be things you will not like about him/her. Psychologists refer to this as ambivalence; and it is as normal as blinking your eyes. We tend to hate the one we love. We hate because we love. Like a jewel collector who spots a flaw in a pearl he admires. He will despise the flaw because he loves the pearl. It is because you consider your partner so precious that you dislike his/her faults, even if they are very small. It fact, we all have the uncanny ability to enlarge postage stamp faults into billboard size defects.

These little things—leaving the socks on the floor, the lights on, the gas tank empty, cupboard doors open—can hurt if not properly handled. We can permit these little matters to eat away at our relationship like beetles eat the center out of an oak. Forbearance and forgiveness, springing from Christ-like love, will be needed for any marriage no matter how naturally compatible the partner might be.

The Receiving Side of Giving Love

By now, you may be thinking that I have a pretty drab view of marriage. I have downplayed the role of romantic love. I have elevated commitment and sacrificial love, both on the giving side. Sounds like a "marathon of misery" contest, with a prize going to the couples that endure to the end. No, I am not saying marriage is the best chance to get your name in *Foxe's Book of Martyrs*.

According to Scripture, marriage is more than an endless giving. There is plenty to be received. The invisible bonds that wrap around the two of you will also be constructed out of the rewards as well as the demands of your relationship. Up to this point, I have been trying to make clear that there is no lasting reward without this sacrificial love.

A story I once heard illustrates this, even though I don't believe it really happened: It was one of those "too good to be true" kind. But I do believe the lesson of the story even if I doubt its facts. It involved a man who hated his wife so much he desperately wanted out of the marriage. He described the situation to the divorce lawyer. "Do you hate her that much?" the lawyer questioned. "Yes," the man confirmed his contempt. "Would she like a divorce?" asked the lawyer. "Yes, that would be no problem; she wants out, too," the wife hater said.

"Divorcing her now is not a very wise thing to do," the lawyer advised, conning his client. He then went on to explain his plan. If the man hated her so much, divorcing her would only make her happy. That was hardly a good way to get even. Going back home, he should do everything he could to make his wife love him. Be a perfect husband. "Then, after she is passionately in love with you, file for divorce." Venomous hatred seething in his innards, the husband was ecstatic over this plan. He left the office with a cool determination to put it into effect immediately.

The end of the story is not hard to guess. When his wife responded in love to his generous, thoughtful behavior, he just wasn't about to divorce her. They lived happily ever after.

No, I don't expect you to believe that tale.

The message is certainly powerful, though. You don't really give out genuine love without eventually getting some of it back. Marriage is a wonderfully reciprocal relationship. Jesus Himself affirms that marriage is one of the most intimate of all relationships. "The two will become one," He said. This oneness is a remarkable, satisfying human experience. The kind of love that solidifies into the toughest bond of marriage is primarily constructed after the wedding. And it must be characterized by Christ-likeness. If you cultivate your oneness in this way, the bond will grow richer and stronger.

The Bond of Mature Love

While the Bible recognizes romantic love that just happens, it gives priority to mature love that takes time and experience to grow.

It is the third biblical bond of love. Of Isaac, the Scriptures report that he *"brought her into the tent of his mother Sarah, and he married Rebekah. So she became his wife, and he loved her"* (Genesis 24:67). His love came after marriage.

This more lasting kind of love grows out of the "one flesh" experience. Think of this oneness as a rope that holds you together. Like a rope it has many strands. It includes sex—a powerful bond itself for many couples. It may be the most important strand in the rope.

The anthropologist Desmond Morris explains that the sexual ties of a man and wife are a powerful, legitimate chain between them. Animals do not have this link. No female animal has the desire for sex as does woman. Female animals are only aroused when they are capable of conception. Woman and man alone, among God's creatures, have such a capacity for enjoying sex any time. Morris concludes, from the naturalistic point of view, that there is a reason why humans get so much pleasure from sex. Evolution, he contends, has developed us in this way to keep couples together during the years when they must care for their young.

What Morris concludes from his purely secular point of view, we can claim for biblical reasons. Man has a tremendous desire to "cleave unto his wife," and woman has great desire toward her husband. God created this his and her sexual urge to keep us from loneliness. Therefore, couples should feel free to allow the sensual bond to keep their relationship tight. They should not feel ashamed or embarrassed because the sexual side of marriage is so great and makes them want to stay together. It was meant to be.

The physical oneness is only one strand in the "one flesh" rope. In fact, the sexual coupling is a symbol of the broader union. We get a picture of the richness of the marriage relationship throughout Scripture. In the Song of Songs marriage is portrayed as deeply personal, sensual, and emotional. To him she is *"darling and beautiful"*; her *"voice is sweet"* and her *"face lovely."* In her eyes he is handsome and pleasant; her *"lover"* and her *"friend"* (Song of Songs 2:14; 5:16).

The Old Testament prophets compared God's love to a husband's love. That is how much they thought of the greatness of the marriage relationship. As the husband of Israel, God says: *"Though the mountains be shaken and the hills be removed, yet my unfailing love for you will not be shaken"* (Isaiah 54:10). And the Apostle Paul carries the idea into the New Testament. He compares the union of Christ and the church to that of a husband and wife (Ephesians 5:22-33).

Marriage, then, is a bonding together of two persons. Their bodies and lives are linked in a unique way to equal one of the greatest of human experiences.

Making Marriage Happen

You have to make marriage happen. Becoming one flesh doesn't just occur when you climb into bed for the first time. Your assignment is to build a marriage that just won't quit. And if you will pardon the expression, that will take work. As a nationally known executive said: "All planning degenerates into work." The idea that a good marriage will just happen is a damaging piece of luggage too many couples take along on their honeymoon. It's a major contemporary misunderstanding.

In her candid article, "Death of a Marriage," Barbara Spence admits she and her husband were plugged into this notion.

> My mother and father have an ideal marriage. Their love for each other was so strong that I assumed marriage was that way for everyone. I was never exposed to any of the work that held their marriage together. It just *was*. I expected mine to be the same. Right before we were divorced, my husband said to me, "Marriage should not have to be work. You fall in love, get married and that's it." He was partly right. You get married and that's it, but now I know that that is when the work begins.[2]

Committed love is the essence of marriage—it includes a promise to work together at building "oneness." I have traveled to scores of places in North America telling this message. After giving it, I always have more than one couple come to me and say "keep sharing these truths." They are usually older couples who then add, "We have a fantastic relationship; but it didn't come easy, just like you have said."

These people were not unfaithful to their marriage. A person can be unfaithful in marriage even though he/she never touched another person in a sexual way. Unfaithfulness is not something you merely do outside of marriage; it is something you don't do inside of marriage. Being faithful is not only avoiding an affair with a third party; it involves cultivating an affair with your own partner. That is what this book is designed to help you do.

Commune Occasion

Sharing About Christ-like Love

The following list of words are those the Bible uses to explain the meaning of sacrificial love. The meaning of each aspect of love is given on pages of this chapter. Use this list to affirm and support each other as Christ-like lovers by following the suggestions that come after the list.

Love:

Is patient
Is kind
Does not envy
Does not boast, is not proud
Is not rude
Is not self-seeking
Is not easily angered
Keeps no record of wrongs
Does not delight in evil, but rejoices with the truth
Bears all things (NASB)
Always trusts
Always hopes
Always perseveres
Never fails

Share

- Which two characteristics of love you most see expressed by your partner.
- Which two characteristics of love you yourself want more of in your own life.

Pray a prayer of thanksgiving for the love God has given you and then ask Him to work in each other's lives where you most need it.

Understanding Your Love.

There have been numerous attempts to describe love between a man and woman, some poetic and some scientific. The following list is given by an author who has had a great deal of experience in working with young adults.[3] He also draws upon the literature on this subject.

Use this list to interact together about the quality of your love for each other. As you do so, keep in mind the following:

● This list is idealistic. Not all of these elements will be in everyone's experience.

● This list deals with "courtship love." It describes the experience of true love, particularly during the early years of a relationship. The qualities can still be found with a couple years later, though.

● This list is practical. You can use the list to determine the direction your love should take. The author, Herbert Miles, reminds us that a couple can grow in this type of love. "These conditions do not happen in a minute or by blind accident," he writes. "They are the result of a careful process of intelligent association, thinking, planning, dialogue, prayer, and divine leadership."[4]

1. You will be concerned about your physical appearance (dressing and grooming) and your personal conduct. One day a boy said to me, "Every time I am with her, she inspires me to be a better person."

2. You will have faith and trust in that person.

3. You will really not have a desire to date other people. Those whom you once thought you loved will recede into the background and into insignificance. Love, necessary for marriage, should be pure, confident, thorough, total and complete.

4. You will want to see, to meet, and to know this person's parents, brothers, sisters, relatives, and friends. You will be anxious to please them. You will be concerned about the well-being of those near and dear to the one you love.

5. You will delight in the personal accomplishments of the person you love. You will not be jealous of that person's achievements.

6. You will have respect for the one you love. You will respect that person's beliefs, values, moral standards, rights, and needs. You will respect that person as a person, a total person.

7. You will have a feeling of inner security as a result of your love for that person. You will feel self-confident, relaxed, and happy even in the face of major personal, social, or financial problems.

8. You will be lonely when circumstances force you to be separated. It will be difficult for you to keep your thoughts and dreams off your lover. You will long for the day and hour when you can be together again.

9. You will sacrifice for the person you love in many different ways. . . . Love is an outgoing something. It is possible for a person to give without loving, but it is impossible to love without giving!

10. You will be hurt when your sweetheart is hurt or criticized. You will rush to the defense of your lover.

11. You will want this person to become, in marriage, the father or mother of your children.

12. You can honestly say that your interest in this person is not simply a physical attraction, a sexual interest, but rather, your interest is in the total person, as a complete personality, involving every aspect of life. To be sure, to be in love with a person includes physical attraction and sexual interest in marriage. This is a major aspect of love. . . . Sex is a part of true love, but it is the servant of all other personal and personality relationships.

13. Other people will know that you are in love. It is nearly impossible for a person in love to keep it a secret.

ENDNOTES

[1]Ann Landers, Field Newspaper Syndicate, *Chicago Sun-Times.*
[2]Barbara Spence, "Death of a Marriage." By permission from His, student magazine of Inter-Varsity Christian Fellowship, © 1980.
[3]Herbert J. Miles, *The Dating Game* (Grand Rapids: Zondervan Publishing House, 1975), pp. 20-22. Used by permission.
[4]*Ibid.,* p. 22.

CHAPTER THREE

ONE PLUS ONE EQUALS ONE
DEVELOPING INTIMACY IN MARRIAGE

Told you would live in a box for the rest of your life, you would be forced to fire a lot of questions at somebody. How big is it? What's the ventilation like? Are there any windows?

Yet we humans get "boxed in" this thing called marriage without asking some of the basic questions about it, like "What is marriage?"

Of course, marriage is what you make it. For both of you. But your ideas of marriage will shape the kind of marriage you build. Knowing what you really think of marriage is very important to constructing marriage. When two people have different or vague ideas about what they are building, it creates problems. Imagine two carpenters erecting a house, each with an entirely different set of blueprints. The result would be confusion . . . and no house.

What Is Marriage, Anyway?

The chances of a couple sharing the same blueprints for marriage are rather slim. This is partly due to the fact that we rarely discuss these matters. We don't ask each other, "What is marriage?" because the answer seems too obvious. After all, there are marriages all around for us to see. Grown people don't go around asking about the obvious. If one adult says to another, "What is a table?

Let's try to agree on a clear definition," you conclude he is either mentally deranged, or a philosopher, or both.

Since marriage is such a household word, we don't often think carefully about defining it. We begin to think everyone thinks the same about it. Thus when someone says, "Will you marry me?" the other person doesn't briskly respond, "Will I what?"

Often the person who asks the question and the one giving the answer believe they are dealing with the same idea. And that is just the problem. Marital trouble usually begins when couples clash over each other's ideas of what they've gotten into.

In her head, for example, marriage is long evenings talking and laughing together, sharing a close relationship. For him, marriage is having sex, having a house, having kids, having gourmet meals, having everything but a close relationship. He gets all of these and thinks he has a "great" marriage. She doesn't get her intimate talks and closeness and feels she has very little marriage at all.

Without agreement, frustration sets in for one or the other, causing one or both to give up the ideals brought into the marriage. Too often they both then settle for a mediocre relationship. They are like the farmer who tried so hard to become an accomplished archer. After weeks of practice without hitting the bull's-eye, he finally shot an arrow into the side of the barn and then drew the target around it.

Too many married people eventually give up. They settle for less because trying to achieve more is just not worth the effort. After years of marriage they finally settle down, fighting disappointment and sorrow, muttering to themselves, "So this is marriage."

A Dim View of Marriage

Complicating the whole defining process is the fact that unconsciously many moderns suspect marriage is not really what it is cracked up to be. Though weddings are such happy affairs, though brides and bridegrooms are so full of anticipation—this doubt exists. Like some demon lurking underneath the altar and under the skirted table that gaily bears the decorated wedding cake, the dark, dismal feeling arises in a couple: They begin to discover marital land is not really Disneyland after all.

Western culture has had a dim view of marriage throughout its history. I discovered this recently when I was preparing a talk for my son's wedding. Since Larry had been a very bright English major in college, I wanted to sprinkle my brief message with some quotations about marriage from the literary giants. Yet I found that finding some good words about marriage in quotation books is as tough as finding good news in the morning paper.

I discovered lots of humorous statements. For example, do you know who said, "The best marriage I can think of is between a blind woman and a deaf man"? And I found some very dismal statements about the marriage state. But I could not find three usable positive statements about marriage from three large books of quotations from the great literature of the western world. Marriage has been receiving bad press for centuries. It started with the Greeks. The Greek poet Palladas said, "Marriage brings a man only two happy days; the day he takes his bride to bed, and the day he lays her in the grave."[1]

Hiding maliciously behind our good notions about marriage is the suspicion that marriage, whatever it is, is something we must learn to grin and bear.

Marriage Defined . . . Biblically

As we have already seen, the Bible contains a very high view of marriage. The Apostle Paul proclaimed that it was created by God and is therefore good (1 Timothy 4:3, 4). In fact, Paul maintains that it is false prophets who bad-mouth marriage.

The nearest we can come to a biblical definition of marriage is the statement from Genesis 2:24 that Jesus quoted: *"For this cause a man shall leave his father and his mother, and shall cleave to his wife; and they shall become one flesh"* (NASB).

Becoming one flesh obviously refers to the sexual union. A man and a woman will have a God-given, powerful drive to be united sexually. I have never read a theologian who defined "one flesh" only in sensual terms, though. Sexual oneness is one of the unique features of marriage; but it is not the only unique aspect.

The significance of the words "one flesh" is found in the context of the passage where they occur. Chapter 2 of Genesis portrays the occasion for the creation of woman. The way the Bible tells it, the creation of Eve is a sort of surprise party. *"So the Lord God formed from the soil every kind of animal and bird, and brought them to*

*the man to see what he would call them; and whatever he called
them, that was their name. But still there was no proper helper for
the man"* (v. 19, 20, TLB).

After finding that none of the creatures already created by
God could be a *"proper helper for the man,"* God constructs such
a person from one of Adam's ribs. *"Then the Lord God caused the
man to fall into a deep sleep, and took one of his ribs and closed
up the place from which he had removed it, and made the rib into
a woman, and brought her to the man"* (v. 21, 22, TLB).

There is a dramatic quality in the last phrase: *"and brought her
to the man."* The first human female is being led down the path
toward the very spot where a man's eyes will first fall upon a woman.
At this point the storyteller has seized our attention as securely as
the naked Eve has captured Adam's. Our eager curiosity is brought
to its peak by the phrase: *"And the man said, . . . "* (Genesis 2:23a,
NASB).

If you permit your imagination to soar, you can have lots of
fun with this. For example: "And Adam said: 'You're the only girl
in the world for me.' "

The story is arranged in such a way as to place heavy emphasis
on Adam's verbal response at the sight of Eve, filling his words with
extraordinary significance.

> *"This is now bone of my bones,*
> *And flesh of my flesh;*
> *She shall be called Woman,*
> *Because she was taken out of Man"* (Genesis 2:23,
> NASB).

Moses, the author of Genesis, then draws a conclusion from
these words: *"For this cause a man shall leave his father and his
mother, and shall cleave to his wife; and they shall become one
flesh. And the man and his wife were both naked and were not
ashamed"* (v. 24, 25, NASB). Eve is created in such a way as to
enable her to become "one flesh" with Adam in the marital
embrace.

The full significance of the creation of Eve cannot be seen
without going back to the reason. Earlier the Lord said, *"It is not
good for the man to be alone; I will make him a helper suitable for
him"* (2:18, NASB). Sex and marriage along with the woman are

created for man to overcome his aloneness. Man needs companionship. Though he is in communion with God, he still needs a relationship with others like himself. Companionship with the divine does not eliminate the need for companionship with others.

Throughout church history there have been those who have suggested that fellowship with God is enough. Monks and hermits have retreated into isolation to cultivate their relationship with God. Pietists have argued that marriage and sex distract from the joyous communion with the inner Christ. As Lewis Smede has said so well: "Some Christians feel that their sexuality is nature's strongest competition for their loyalty to Christ. 'You cannot love God and sex.'"

Companionship in marriage need not be opposed to fellowship with God, however. Man needs both human and divine relationships. If Adam was alone in paradise, how much more is it possible in Pasadena—in our large, modern, depersonalized existence.

Marriage Is a Blender

Marriage is best described as oneness; it is a unique physical oneness, a union of bodies. What's more, it is a unique blending of persons. This blending is a deeply personal, interpersonal relationship, a fact clearly demonstrated from the Scriptures. "They were both naked and were not ashamed" shows that Adam and Eve were emotionally close. Neither fear, embarrassment, nor shame kept them from enjoying the intimate sight, sounds, and touch of the other. Our fear and shame over sharing our naked bodies, sexual responses, and personal inward selves is not part of God's creation; that comes after sin cuts us off from one another.

In marriage, two persons unshamefully learn of one another. For this reason the Hebrews used the word "to know" when speaking of sexual intercourse. This is not just a nice way of talking about sex in public and in front of little kids. It reveals that those in the Old Testament viewed marriage as a deeply interpersonal experience.

Even the Hebrew word "flesh" supports the idea that marriage is not just a union of bodies. The word can be used when speaking of the whole person, which shows that "one flesh" means a union of two people.

This companionship idea of marriage is also found in the words that describe Adam's wife. She is called a *"helper suitable for him."* This phrase may refer to the fact that she will help him overcome his aloneness. It also refers to the fact that she will help Adam face the duties and experiences of his life. They are to share life together.

Marriage then can be considered to be an intimate sharing: a sharing of bodies, of selves, of experiences. Such sharing is to be intimate, because it involves the intertwining of the inner worlds as well as the external selves.

The Brand Name of the Marriage Blender Is "Intimacy"

From a biblical standpoint, marriage cannot be reduced to a mere sharing of the same bed or the same house. Two people can live in the same rooms, use the same bathroom, have sexual intercourse, and still come short of the kind of human companionship God intended. Fear, selfishness, and shame can keep them from entering into a close personal union. Even though married, they still remain alone, united only in part.

This ancient biblical notion of marriage is surprisingly what we moderns are still after. The contemporary interest in sex can be traced to a greater interest in intimacy.

When McCall's magazine asked women the question: "What is most important to you now?" 61% of the 20,000 replied: "A feeling of being close to someone." Surveyer Daniel Yankelovich said that *Playboy* magazine was surprised to discover most men felt the same way. The ideal lover chosen by the majority of men interviewed was "someone I could be totally open and honest with." Sexual titillation, physical pleasure, and virtuoso performance in bed played a subordinate role to intimacy.

This idea of marriage as intimacy is the major theme of this book. Therefore, the rest of the book will deal with these dynamics of intimate life.

But there are several things to be understood about intimacy which are crucial to your achieving it. Intimacy is both deep and wide. It is deep in that it demands the sharing of one's inner self—allowing another to explore the inner caverns of self. Sexual intercourse symbolizes this by the sharing of the body's personal and private parts, and responses. Marital intimacy goes further than sexual exchanges when there is an unveiling of one's very personal thoughts and feelings.

Intimacy is also wide. The exploration includes the *physical:* the touch of each other's bodies; the color of her eyes; the sound of his voice; the warmth of physical closeness; the *emotional:* making each other laugh; standing by while one cries; enduring the other's angry outburst; being bored or depressed together; the *intellectual:* discussing a book you have each read; sharing your concept of God; arguing about political views; discussing new ideas; the *social:* liking the same people; having a long talk with another couple; meeting with a small group; going to a party; the *spiritual:* sharing our highest longings; committing ourselves to certain values; worshiping at church and as a couple; praying about personal matters in the other's presence.

Intimacy Is Both Communication and Companionship

Intimacy will require developing *both* your communication and your companionship. Intimacy is not just talking together; it is also doing together. The talking and the doing enhance one another. A couple can enjoy deep intimacy during a quiet walk by a lake, though no words are exchanged.

Intimacy therefore includes developing areas of your life like *recreation:* playing or seeing a game and sharing the joy of winning and the agony of defeat; leisurely engaging in the same hobby; *creation:* redecorating the bedroom; refinishing a chair; building something together; *serving:* teaching a Sunday school class together; working on a fund drive; volunteering for inner city ministry; working to get a political candidate into office.

Intimacy from Communication

Doing these things together makes a great contribution to your intimate experience. This is partly true because it provides the necessary time intimacy requires. Doing things together will force you to be together and to talk.

Ginger and I have learned this through our Tuesday nights out. For years we have scheduled Tuesday night just for the two of us. With four children around the house, counting on finding an uninterrupted hour together is like counting on finding a can of pop in the refrigerator. The solution: a night out a week.

And both of us relish the anticipation of our special Tuesday evenings. All week long I think of things I want to discuss at length with Ginger. I have been surprised by what happens.

We climb into our car, drive off to a restaurant, park, or other place to be together, and find ourselves accompanied by a strange silence. Neither of us feels like talking. Eventually we begin to share. By the time we are finished with the salad we have exchanged some words about the kids, the bills, and various things. With dessert comes some more significant personal conversation. Usually by the end of the evening we have exposed something of our thoughts and feelings in a meaningful way. We have learned from this that it takes time to get close.

Marriage is like a growing apart and then coming together again—apartness then closeness, etc. Paul Tournier maintains that significant talk must be preceded by small talk. And small talk can be generated by our sharing in life's activities together. Couples who have little time together are handicapped in playing the game of intimacy. You can't build a marriage without the help of the clock.

Intimacy from Activities Together

Activities together give us a chance to see into each other better and then approve of what we see. Such affirmation is necessary to successful intimacy. We want a person to accept the part of the self we expose to them. When we share activities together we communicate acceptance and that brings us very close.

I felt this once when I was showing Ginger a beautiful place I had seen. When we moved to Chicago, people urged us to visit a college and seminary campus near our community. After months of driving by this campus called St. Mary of the Lake, I heeded their advice and drove through the gate. It was all that people had promised it would be: old brick colonial styled buildings, surrounded by deep woods, patches of cultivated flowers and shrubbery, rabbits and squirrels scampering across the miles of winding roads through the trees that sat on the edge of a calm blue lake. I was impressed.

My initial emotions included the desire to share this beauty with my Ginger. Soon after, one lazy Sunday afternoon provided the opportunity. When we drove onto the campus I watched for her reaction. Her usual enthusiastic repertoire of words didn't fail her now. "Oh, that's beautiful," "Look at those fantastic trees,"

"This place is gorgeous," she repeated as we drove slowly through that colorful wonderland.

The words that leapt from her mouth caused my heart to jump. We were being drawn closer and closer by our mutual delight. Not only was she affirming the beauty of that place, she was identifying with my feelings and approving them.

If you think of the opposite reaction, it will make this point more clear. Suppose she had said, "Oh, this is O.K., but I've seen lots of places that would make this look like an empty lot." Her rejection of that place would have equaled a rejection of me, of my tastes and feelings.

So when a wife says: "I can't understand why you like to shoot pool; what a foolish thing to do," or a husband says, "How can you possibly stand listening to that symphony music?" they damage their relationship. Intimacy is made by trying to understand what each other feels, thinks, and experiences.

We should discover those activities that delight both of us, so that we can use them as occasions to know and affirm one another. One woman told me of how she saved her marriage by doing this. In this case, the husband was not willing to take time to do with her what she enjoyed. He was caught up in restoring old cars. When it became evident his endless hours in the garage were tearing their relationship apart, she made her decision. Donning a pair of coveralls, she entered the garage, crawled under a car beside her husband, pointed to what he was working on and said, "What's that?" He described the transmission to her and she permitted him to turn her into an automobile nut like himself. Now the endless hours together in the garage restoring old cars have revitalized their relationship.

A Goal Not Easily Achieved

The realization that such intimacy is not easily achieved is another important thing to understanding about it. The greatest illusion about intimacy is the false idea that it is easy. Two consenting adults crawl into a sleeping bag to share their naked bodies beside some romantic lake, having met several hours before, and believe they have achieved "instant intimacy." In reality, unveiling each other's body is actually easier than disclosing each other's true self. An expert in this area, Andrew Greeley, makes this point forcefully.

"Intimacy, then, is always difficult, and when it stops being difficult it stops being intimacy," he claims.[2]

The difficulty of getting truly close to one another is rooted in our sinfulness. Sin has not only separated us from God, but also from each other. It is the source of suspicion, shame, guilt, anger, and rejection; all of which make intimacy difficult, if not impossible.

Because intimacy is difficult to achieve, marriage will require a great deal of patience as you each grow more accustomed to it. Erik Erikson maintains that learning the dynamics of intimacy is one of the major tasks of the person between ages twenty and forty.

Allow intimacy to unfold in your marriage without forcing or demanding harshly. Becoming critical of a partner who is reluctant to disclose himself will only make it more difficult for him or her to do so. Intimacy thrives in an uncritical attitude of acceptance. Whether it is sexual, emotional, intellectual, or any other kind of intimacy, you cannot force it to happen. Intimacy will grow like a house plant when the atmosphere and conditions permit it to do so.

Intimate but Individual

One further understanding of marital intimacy is crucial: Intimacy should not destroy your individuality. Though a man and wife become one flesh, they each also exist as individuals. When you grow together as a couple, you will also need to be free to grow as an individual. Though you cannot get too much of positive intimacy, you can allow your intimacy to squelch the other person and deny his or her freedom.

Andrew Greeley warns about getting too close.

"Intimacy in marriage can be oppressively close. It can take on the inevitability of a soggy, humid summer day or a bitter winter's snowstorm. One is simply caught up in it; you cannot enjoy it, you cannot escape from it. The relationship is intricate, complex, subtle, powerful, demanding, and occasionally rewarding, of course."[3]

In your pursuit of intimacy, then, you will need to guard each other's personal need for individual freedom to grow. The cultivating of your individual life will enable you to bring enrichment to each other whenever you share. Your closeness will not come about by smothering, but by uniting. At those times when intimacy becomes too oppressive, you will need to back off a bit before coming back for more intense involvement.

Commune Occasion
Looking at Our Intimate Experience

Choose your answers to the following multiple choice questions, then discuss them. Note: this is not a test of your understanding of the chapter. Though I am a teacher, I would not do this to you. Instead, it is a chance to share your own attitudes and ideas in regard to intimacy.

1. When the Bible speaks of marriage as a "one flesh" relationship, I think mostly of:

   a. The sexual relationship.
   b. Having children.
   c. A very close relationship.
   d. A permanent relationship.

2. When I think of intimacy, I think of (choose three):

   a. Walking in the woods together.
   b. Sharing secrets with each other.
   c. Physical touching.
   d. Serving others together.
   e. Long conversations.
   f. Playing a game together.
   g. Knowing what a person thinks before they say it.

3. Reasons why it is hard to be intimate include:

   a. Fear of whether or not you will be accepted.
   b. People are too busy.
   c. People don't really want it.
   d. The way persons grew up, making it hard to reveal themselves.
   e. Our independent attitudes.
   f. Fear of losing our own identities.

g. Fear of being dominated by someone.

4. If I were to select areas where I would like us to grow in our own communication intimacy, they would be:

   a. Sharing of how we feel when we feel good.
   b. Sharing of how we feel when we feel bad or upset.
   c. Sharing of ideas.
   d. Sharing of inner thoughts.
   e. Just more talking about anything.
   f. Sharing of romantic statements.
   g. Sharing about spiritual things.
   h. Sharing about what happened in our past lives.

5. If I were to select areas where I would like us to grow in our companionship intimacy, they would be (choose two):

   a. Playing together.
   b. Physical touching.
   c. Serving others/God together.
   d. Creating something together (a hobby, for example).
   e. Working together.
   f. Serving some cause together.
   g. Sharing music, art, or other beautiful things together in appreciation.

ENDNOTES

[1]Morton Hunt, *The Natural History of Love* (New York: Alfred Knopf, 1958), p. 58.

[2]Andrew Greeley, *Sexual Intimacy* (Chicago: The Thomas More Press, 1973), p. 26.

[3]Andrew Greeley, *Love and Play* (Chicago: The Thomas More Press, 1975), p. 23.

CHAPTER FOUR

AMALGAMATION, NOT ANNIHILATION
MAKING DIFFERENCES WORK FOR OUR MARRIAGES

Things that go together are often very much different: peaches and cream, a violin and a bow, a horse and a carriage. Some of these things have been used to illustrate marriage: a lock and a key, and a violin and a bow, particularly.

The Bible makes it clear that oneness in marriage results from the union of opposites. It is two halves becoming one whole. The wholeness is possible because the halves are partially different. When God created the woman for Adam, she had to be somewhat like him: *"Bone of his bones and flesh of his flesh."* But she also qualified because she was different: a *"helper suitable for him."* The word "suitable" meant she was opposite to him. Being Adam's sexual opposite, female, she could couple with him, the male.

Interestingly, when God made a helper for Adam to overcome his aloneness, he did not choose to make another man. No doubt the major reason was the biological one: He wanted the first pair to populate the earth. However, it is possible that there is something more to the male-female distinction than that.

Apparently God made a woman for the male because for humanity to be true humanity, there must be two sexes. The influential theologian, Karl Barth, even concluded that in order for man to be in the image of God, he would need to be both male and female. He referred to the verse, Genesis 1:27, where the idea of the image of God is related to maleness and femaleness. *"So God created man in his own image, in the image of God He created him; male and female He created them."*

Barth's view is probably incorrect, since any individual is said to be in God's image, not a couple. Yet, there does seem to be some reason for God's making the male-female distinctions apart from the purpose of reproduction. Man and woman, and the differences between them, have something to do with a complete idea of humanity. And it is because of these differences that they can become one. Therefore, marriage is a blending of two different persons.

See Each Other as Different, Not Odd

This concept of marriage demands that each of you learn to accept the differences of the other. This is one of the great joys of marriage: learning to receive and know fully a person different from myself.

Too often these dissimilarities drive us apart because one of us doesn't allow the other to be himself. One begins to dominate; the other feels threatened and crushed. Many times it happens like the old joke portrays: "As the couple is coming down the aisle, after the ceremony, someone says, 'They are one now. It's just a matter of time before we will know which one they have become.' " True oneness, though, results from an amalgamation of two, not an annihilation of one.

It is all too easy for us to reject the other partner's differences. We can easily begin to compete with each other, failing to recognize that a strength that one of us has is a strength for both of us.

Couples argue over who has the best memory for detail. "It happened on a Thursday," she says. "I distinctly remember it was after your birthday, which was on a Wednesday." "No," he retorts, "it happened on a Friday; it was the day before I went to play golf with Fred." Sometimes the competition is friendly. It can become more critical and destructive.

You can allow these differences to work for, not against you. Not long after our marriage, I learned that Ginger's memory for everyday details was far superior to mine. While I did compete during the first years of marriage, I soon learned that it was not much of a contest since she was right ninety-eight percent of the time. Now, I have learned to appreciate this quality in her. Whenever we have to move a sofa out of the house, for example, I can go to her for help. She usually remembers which door we brought it in and even how we turned it to get it through the doorway.

Differences, I have learned, can make our marriage stronger, if we react to them properly.

See Differences as a Chance to Love

These differences also provide a great opportunity for loving and caring. One of the most gracious things we can do for one another is to understand each other as male and female.

Ginger told me how hard it was during the early years of marriage to deal with certain feminine traits that she had. She feared I would not understand her regular depression caused by her monthly menstrual cycle. She tried to cover her moodiness, avoiding me during certain periods. And yet she longed to go to me and explain and have me comfort her. But because she feared rejection, and perhaps because I gave her cause for such fear, she kept her inner sadness to herself.

One day she got the courage to share with me how she really felt. Instead of treating her harshly, I said I understood. Now she tells me how comforting it is to come and request, "I'm really feeling down; can I have your shoulder to cry on?" I consider these choice opportunities to show my love to her—to say, I accept you, despite our differences.

See Your Differences as a Complement

Two different beings becoming one means we should not fear asserting ourselves, too. Only when the two parts of the whole are truly what they were meant to be can the oneness be made possible. Each needs the other like a lock needs a key. This is especially true in the sexual realm where the man's sexuality is dependent upon the female's sexual response and vice versa.

The need of one for the other is true in other realms. For this reason one theologian says of marriage: "One plus one equals three." Each of you brings a strength to the marriage. When you assert yourself you strengthen the whole. If you hold back, you may deny the two of you what is crucial to your marriage.

Sometimes we will fail to assert ourselves because we fear conflict or feel rejection. Or, often we will hold back because we are somewhat weary of doing our part. We wish the other person would not be so dependent. We shrink from our responsibility. In some cases this causes overwhelming problems because the differences are what make the couple fall in love in the first place.

We know that people often marry people who are psychologically opposites of themselves. Persons who are outgoing often marry socially quiet persons; a man or woman who is highly disciplined will often marry someone who is undisciplined. The reason is obvious. The one helps the other.

For example, if she is depressive and he is lighthearted, he helps her with her down moods. Depressed again, she sits in her dormitory room wondering how she can make it through the evening. Then she hears his Suzuki coming down the street and her sadness begins to lift.

When she meets him at the door, she says: "I'm really down tonight." Not letting it faze him, he invites her to hop on and off they go for an evening of mirth that has her laughing as she walks back into her dorm room. How she loves him; like no one else, he has brought happiness into her life.

The pattern of their interaction looks like this:

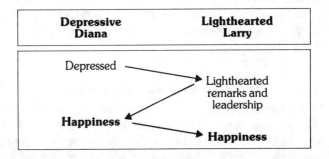

Depressive Diana	Lighthearted Larry
Depressed ⟶	Lighthearted remarks and leadership
Happiness ⟵	**Happiness**

Sadly, marriage can turn these opposite traits into irritations. The responses and reactions change. We begin to resent the other person for being what they are. The thing that made us love them now makes us mad.

Take our example of Diana and Larry. After marriage, Larry walks into the house to find Diana depressed for the fourth time that week. Now he is tired of pulling her out. So he reacts this time with hostility.

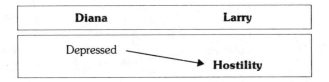

Diana now reacts to a husband who is different from the man she married. Though he was capable of hostility, he had never reacted that way before. And so she reacts in her way to a person who is hostile: She withdraws, locking herself in the bathroom.

The pattern:

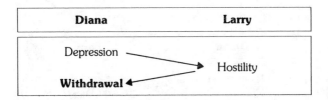

It is Larry's turn to react at this point. When people withdraw from him, he does the same to them. He goes outside and rides his motorcycle for a couple of hours.

The pattern is now like this:

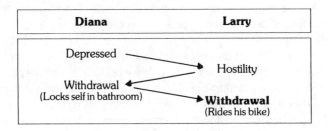

When people withdraw from her, Diana frantically tries to win them back. Thus she continues to try to restore the relationship and bring the withdrawing husband into her inner circle. This gets frustrating as the months of reaction/interaction continue. When frustrated, she eats and gains weight. The pattern has now become:

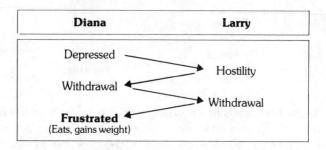

And now, lighthearted Larry will react. Her gain of weight takes the fun out of life and he gets depressed.

Thus:

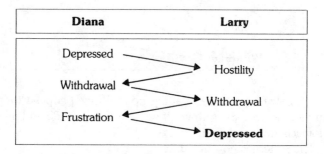

And of course, when Larry gets depressed, Diana does. And the pattern ends with two depressed people in a depressed relationship.

In this case, what Larry should realize is that he needs to continue to successfully live with a wife who suffers from depression. Changing his reaction to hostility instead of helpfulness put them into a damaging pattern. He needs to accept his wife's difference and assert his own lighthearted temperament. While it is true that Diana must not depend only upon Larry to help her with her moods, Larry's hostile reaction is not what she needs. She needs his continual understanding and joyfulness.

The pattern of interaction for this couple is all too common. It occurs because the differences we accepted before marriage are now no longer tolerated. Yet, marriage is based upon the unity of two distinct persons. Living in marriage means learning to live with someone blissfully and sometimes painfully different from ourselves.

Commune Occasion

Discussing Our Differences and the Difference They Make.

The "Wow! You're Something Else" Interchange:

1. Each of you make a list of five ways your partner is different from you that you really like.

    1.
    2.
    3.
    4.
    5.

2. Each of you share one at a time with each other.

The Male-female Differences:

1. Each of you think of some of the major ways you perceive the other to be different because you are male and female. You may disagree that there are many such differences, apart from the physical, which is fine. But the important thing is to help each other become more aware of what you are like. For example, if as a woman, you do have times of the month when you are especially moody, you will want your husband to understand how you feel and why.
2. Each of you now share one at a time with each other.

The Temperamental Togetherness:

Look at each of the following descriptions of temperament to see if you perceive any difference between the two of you in that characteristic. Then discuss whether or not the difference makes your personalities harmonious in that area or if it is a source of irritation.

Lighthearted, joyful attitude.
Tends toward depression and moodiness.

Very disciplined.

Rather easygoing, struggling for self-control.

Very tolerant of other people.

Intolerant of others.

Outgoing; loves to be with people much of the time.

More withdrawn; loves to be alone with a good book or something.

Very expressive of thoughts and emotions.

Rather inhibited in sharing feelings and internal ideas.

Very aggressive in wanting to get things done; a leader.

Rather easygoing; not pushing to accomplish; a follower.

CHAPTER FIVE

MARRIAGE OR MIRAGE? HOW TO SHARE THE REAL YOU

When I close my eyes, I can still see her face and hear her words. The young college girl I stood before had just been told that her father had suddenly died. We were at a summer camp in the mountains near Los Angeles. As the speaker of the week, I had been asked to accompany the pastor who met with the girl to tell her of the telephone call that had brought the dreaded news. We stood by while she wept; then, her composure regained, she verbalized the regret that must have been at the forefront of her initial inner thoughts, "My father, my father; I never really knew him."

How tragic. Surely a daughter has a right to know her father. Many times people keep themselves from one another—in the family and in marriage. "Arnold, you are such a wonderful husband," said a wife. "But I still can't help wondering what you are really like."

Many relationships are deceptions. We hide our real self, fearing to disclose who we really are. Surely most people enter marriage believing it will be different for them. After all, their communication is already spectacular. One engaged man, a student of mine, said his newly-developed relationship was uncanny. "I can actually read her mind. She will sit quietly in my presence and I will say something and she will say in utter surprise: 'That is just what I was thinking.' "

Communication is not that simple, though, even for those who are deeply in love. "I live on an island, and he lives on an island, and neither of us can swim," quipped one person, expressing the frustration so many of us feel.

It comes in part because of our fear of intimacy. We are cowardly about letting ourselves out of the bag because it is very uncomfortable. We are afraid we will be rejected. Or else we fear what we say or confess will be used against us someday.

The Meaning of Self-disclosure

Self-disclosure is basic to companionship in marriage. We must overcome our fears and make it comfortable for each of us to express and be himself.

Self-disclosure: Not Lung to Tongue

Self-disclosure is such a worn term today that I want to be careful about its meaning. When I use the term self-disclosure, I do not mean impulsiveness. Sometimes couples want a marriage where the vocal cords should vibrate to any and every thought that comes to the mind. They confuse being spontaneous with being impulsive.

Some people use the idea of honesty to justify their impulsiveness. John McEnroe, for example, by his own admission, is likely to get upset on the tennis court, as he did at Wimbledon in 1981. *Newsweek* and scores of reporters commented on his towering tantrums and indefensible insults. When asked about this later, he defended himself as an open person. "I am no hypocrite; people know where I stand. I believe we should be out front with each other and be honest."

However, he was fined and greatly criticized for his uncontrolled outbursts. He called one official an incompetent fool . . . and accused another of racial bias. Letting off steam with such slanderous remarks should not be justified by naming it openness. The blanket of authenticity cannot be used to cover abusive speech and impulsive actions.

A spontaneous person is fun to be with—freely sharing feelings and thoughts in a sincere, enthusiastic reaction to life. Even a genuinely spontaneous person learns to curb his speech, though. Control of the tongue is a mark of Christian maturity, according to James. And Paul cautions us to speak a word that is good for building up others (Ephesians 4:29).

Persons who impulsively go from "the lung to the tongue" in the name of self-disclosure usually don't have many friends, according to the social scientists. And while you will want an honest marriage, you will know that an impulsive transparency will not always be loving. Lawrence Crabb warns against this:

> If we asked people to define an intimate relationship, most in our feeling-oriented culture would suggest that an intimate relationship is one in which they can share everything they feel. . . . There are times in relationships built around mutual ministry in which one part will choose not to share certain feelings . . . because holding in his feelings furthers the purposes of God. . . . A depressed husband should simply push his depression on the back burner when his wife is boiling from the pressure of three kids and a dirty house.[1]

Self-disclosure: Not Raw Nakedness

Nor do I want to define self-disclosure as "psychological nakedness." The intention we have to tell everything and anything about ourselves and our thoughts is good, but it must not be carried too far or too fast. It is taken too far when it is compulsive, when the urge to share is based on a fear of aloneness.

All of us must learn to develop an inner peace with some knowledge, thoughts, and experiences we cannot share with another human. Death is the most individual experience of all. No companion can share entirely that event with us. (Thank God He is present with us then.)

We must learn to accept the fact that there may be some things we cannot share with our lover. Don't interpret this to mean that we must not share all we can and should. One of the most beautiful love stories I ever heard was told by Charlie Shedd. He explained how he once shared himself with his wife. For hours he wrote a lengthy biography, including every experience, every thought, every feeling he could recall.

Later, on a train trip, sitting beside his wife, he summoned the courage to pull the stack of papers from his briefcase and handed them to her. Silently he sat beside her while her eyes, page by page, stripped him of every pretense, deception, and human veneer, and exposed him to her as he never before was exposed to another. When she finally put the last page down, she turned to him, eyes radiating warmth and acceptance, and said, "Charlie, I love you."

Not many couples are going to choose such an unusual and radical path to self-disclosure. Not many couples' relationships could survive that. I see what Shedd is talking about as a great goal of marriage: a continual self-disclosure of who you are.

Self-disclosure Is Sharing the Unique You

Self-disclosure in marriage means sharing your intimate feelings, inner thoughts, and desires. In short, it means sharing the unique you. John Powell, communication expert, says that you really don't share yourself if you don't share your inner world of feeling. If you share an opinion, "I am against war," there is nothing unique about that. But when you tell how you feel about war and the events of your life that led you to that, you share what is uniquely yours to give.

For example, I could tell you that I love my wife, Ginger. That statement is as novel as a potato salad at a picnic. Now if I scoop some feelings from my inner self and share these, I offer more of myself.

I could explain how I feel about her by comparing my feelings to colors. I feel sometimes like the color yellow when I think of her or am around her. She is bright and cheerful, almost always the optimist, checking out the bright side. When I am with her it is sometimes like being in a room full of sunshine. I also think of her in terms of dark blue or even orange. These tones are the shades of feeling when I am with her in a dim room, privately, when she is mine and I am hers.

We are enveloped together at times, a strong magnetic-like quality pulling us toward one another. Because of this I can understand why poets and songwriters have used words like *magnetic* and *attraction* to speak of love. I feel so good in those moments of extreme closeness when the almost supernatural spiritual powers of love surround us, overflowing from each to the other.

Here, then, is part of what I *feel* about Ginger and our relationship. Granted, these words and emotions are not unique, but they are mine; they do attempt to get closer to the inner me.

The love song of the Bible, the *Song of Songs,* contains

numerous statements of inner feeling. *"You have stolen my heart, my sister, my bride; you have stolen my heart with one glance of your eyes"* (4:9), he says of her. Often, Old Testament writers expressed their feelings in metaphors. When Solomon says *"Your hair is like a flock of goats descending from Mount Gilead"* (4:1b), he may have been describing his feelings more than he was her hair. As an outdoorsman, he was saying: I feel refreshed, happy, when I look at your hair as when I look on one of my flocks at the time of rest toward the end of day.

Self-disclosure is Essential to Intimacy and Love

This sharing is the very essence of intimacy. The Latin word for inner or innermost is *intimus.* Thus, being intimate involves grasping the internal reality of someone; the search for intimacy is a search for the inmost character of the person.

Erich Fromm says that "love is the active penetration of the other person." Marriage is a fusion at a very deep level. We share ourselves as an act of love according to John Powell. Whenever you give yourself in that way to someone and they receive you, love is complete in both the offering and the accepting. The beauty of this is that it is free; it costs no money. The poorest of the world can have this.

This act of inner sharing is one of the major parts of the initial falling in love. The early weeks and months of a new relationship are full of discovery. The more personal we become with each other the more exciting the relationship gets.

Yet, the act of discovery often stops. After a few years, couples often make the mistake of thinking they now know each other. "I can read my wife like a book," he says. Then the excitement goes because the discovering ends.

My favorite writer on intimacy, Andrew Greeley, points out the problem: "Perhaps the greatest weakness in the preparation that young people receive today for marriage is that no one tells them that life together will be and ought to be an ongoing series of surprises, of discoveries made, of sudden and illuminating bursts of understanding and self-revelation. New puzzles, obscurities, and secrets will be ever present to be probed, explored, and understood. To explore the depths of someone else's personality is the most erotic thing a human being can do, and when that exploration is reinforced and facilitated by sexual lovemaking, the lovemaking becomes an episode in a grand adventure, taking on an intensity of pleasure that it would otherwise not have."[2]

Have you ever been amused by a confident husband and wife who state that they know their spouses perfectly? Everyone around them senses that they hardly understand each other at all. They have failed to realize that each is a mystery . . . that marriage is a lifelong unraveling of that person page by page.

I see my wife Ginger as a vast forest; I am the explorer. The more I discover, the more delighted I am by the beauty and intricacy of the territory.

Developing Self-disclosure

Now, how can you have more of it?

Consider the Image Problem

For some, particularly men, the sharing of feelings is a sign of weakness. In our culture, a man is told to keep his feelings to himself. We exalt the image of the cowboy and the playboy.

John Wayne was a picture of two things that went together: strength and silence. Ever hear him say in a movie, "Those Indians sure have me depressed." The modern playboy is also a silent type; he uses women, never getting too close, welcoming a woman into his apartment, but not the inner sanctum of his soul.

The tough male learns to cover up. "Don't cry, be a big boy," echoes in his mind from his past. When facing a deathbed scene in front of the TV, he hides his feelings with humor: "The only reason he is crying is because he has to pay the hospital bill."

But Jesus, the Man, unlike the cowboy and playboy, showed and expressed his feelings. *"My soul is overwhelmed with sorrow to the point of death,"* He said (Matthew 26:38).

We know that most men in marriage overcome this wrong image of a man; their wives usually help them. They soon learn that a woman wants strength, but not silence. She wants courage, but she welcomes confession. She wants someone she can depend upon, but someone who also depends upon her.

Women, perhaps even more than men, love someone for their weaknesses. When a man reveals a weakness, he opens a door into his life for her. She finds an opening to enter and encourage and console. It works both ways, though; we need to let each other in so that we may be helpful; that we may be more truly one.

Overcome the Fears

Our fears of being open are mostly unconscious. Sometimes when we are about to share a very intimate thought, we hesitate, back off and away. It's just hard to do. If you can bring those fears to the surface, you might be able to deal with them. Sometimes fear is related to your own need for privacy. If you share all of yourself, you unconsciously are afraid of somehow losing yourself, your individuality. It will help you to understand that intimacy does not require this.

Howard and Charlotte Clinebell explain that the union of intimacy is always only partial. With it goes a sense of communion—which requires the presence of two individuals joined deeply, but maintaining their individuality. Creative intimacy has respect for needed privacy—one's own and one's partner's—as an indispensable ingredient. You can help each other at this point. We must be careful not to press too hard, demanding too much openness of one another. We should provide the atmosphere for sharing, a climate of freedom. Demands create a pressure chamber in which it is difficult to share oneself.

Another roadblock to sharing is the fear that private information might be used against you. This is almost always mentioned when I ask about fears of self-disclosure in my marriage seminars. If you're afraid your partner will use intimate information against you, your relationship is too competitive. Marriage is a love-match, not a prize-fight. When couples are selfishly fighting each other, they need a tender, Christ-like love that forgives, accepts, and does not seek its own way. In this case, the sharing of feelings is not so much the problem as the basic need for respect and cooperation in marriage.

Talk About Talking

The task of sharing feelings is for both of you. It needs to be worked out together. The best thing you can do for your communication is to communicate about it. Discuss how you would like to share your feelings, and why you might be inhibited. Talk about how you can improve in this area.

You can benefit from talking about your reactions. It is your reaction to each other that will make the difference in whether or not much sharing will take place. Desires, for example, are hard to talk about. They often provoke a bad reaction from our spouse. It may be hard for a wife to share, "I would like to have a home in the country someday." This is not because she doesn't want to share it, but because she wouldn't dare. It might make her husband feel bad that he can't provide it. Or, it might seem like she is pressing him to change jobs.

Ginger and I have always had a problem with window shopping. Stopping by a window, she would say: "Wouldn't that look nice in our hallway." I would often turn away, disinterested, knowing at that price it would never look nice in our hallway. Too often I said the wrong thing: "Honey, we can't afford that." It has taken many years for me to understand she wasn't asking for it. She enjoyed dreaming about decorating our house. Now I try harder to play this window shopping game, knowing the sharing of dreams is one of the joys of intimacy.

Desires are hard to mention in other areas as well. A husband may be reluctant to invite his wife to a lovemaking session; he's afraid she will refuse. She may be reluctant to say she feels like going out for dinner; she's worried he may harshly bring up the budget.

Together, we must work on these kinds of difficulties in communication. We should discuss whether or not it is all right to express our desires. We should talk about how we will refuse one another. In short, we should talk about our talking problems, and how we can improve.

Take Time to Share

A little chorus says, "take time to pray, every day." We know that a relationship to God requires some regular talking, getting down to brass tacks. And that takes time. It takes the same time and effort to maintain a warm relationship with each other. Everyday life tends to force us to talk about the superficial things.

One of my fellow professors with three children complained how the in-depth talk had gone out of his relationship with his wife. Before they were married, they talked of their ideas, convictions, and feelings. Now they talk about problems, food, and money. Once they talked of dreams; now, of diapers. They used to talk about how they were going to change the world; now they discuss how they will manage to make it financially through the month.

To foster more personal sharing, you will have to get in the right mood. And to encourage this mood, you will need to deliberately get away from the everyday distractions where you can concentrate on each other.

Use Some Special Techniques to Share

You can take advantage of the communications revolution in the search for self-disclosure. Most of us know about one part of the revolution: We have developed the media to communicate over long distances. We are not amazed at our capability to watch a tennis match that takes place in another hemisphere. Today's communication advances have touched the area of short distances, too. A great deal of research has gone into finding and untangling the snags in interpersonal communication.

Numerous written communication exercises are now available, similiar to the ones that follow each of the chapters in this book. I have been encouraging couples of all ages to use such exercises. The results are often quite spectacular. Pastors who have taken my course on family life ministry have told me their whole marriage has been remodeled. Frequently I receive comments like: "We understand each other better, even after twenty-five years of marriage."

While some of these exercises are more elaborate, the one suggested in the popular marriage encounter movement is relatively simple to do. The "ten-ten" approach consists of writing for ten minutes and then sharing for ten. Deciding the day before on an area of interest, each partner writes in the form of a love note the answer to a question or two, related to the specified subject.

Questions range over the whole of human experience. "How do I feel about my childhood?" "What feelings do I have when I think of death?" "What are some of the reasons I have self-esteem; what are some of the reasons why I have a hard time liking myself?" "What feelings do I have about the future?" "What does good friendship mean to me?" "If someone insults or wrongs me, I feel . . ." "One of the most difficult areas of interpersonal relationship is . . ."

Many of the couples who have used the "ten-ten" approach talk about it transforming their marriages. Some have even bought new wedding bands to symbolize the new beginning. Before, they seemed like strangers; now they have discovered one another and are continually excited about doing so. Before, they were physically bound, and now they are emotionally united. They have discovered a oneness that moves from exterior association to intimate revelations. They have found intimacy—something marriage promises to those who seek it. Go for it.

Commune Occasion

Sharing Feelings

Choose five of the following you would agree to share with your partner. You should volunteer.

1. A time when I was greatly embarrassed and how I felt.
2. How I feel whenever someone ignores me.
3. How I feel whenever I am in a very large city.
4. How I feel whenever I am in some natural setting, like in the deep woods, by the ocean or a lake, in the mountains, standing by a river, etc.
5. Something I have hardly ever told anyone, but which I would like to tell you.
6. Some of the fears I have when trying to share my feelings.
7. A feeling that is very hard for me to share.
8. A subject I feel embarrassed or uncomfortable discussing.
9. Something about our world that causes me anxiety.
10. How I feel when I think of the grace of God.
11. How I feel whenever I think of my childhood.

Evaluating Our Sharing of Feelings

Evaluate your discussion of the sharing you just did by judging how well you did on each of the following items:

Quite satisfactory				Needs improvement
1	2	3	4	5

_____ Ease in choosing items from the above list
_____ Careful listening to each other
_____ Conveying acceptance to each other while we were sharing
_____ Depth of sharing on each item chosen
_____ Comfort in sharing with each other

Share your evaluation item by item and discuss why you evaluated as you did. Discuss how you can now improve your communication.

ENDNOTES

[1]Gil Peterson, ed., "Manipulation or Ministry," *Family Life Education* (Glen Ellyn, Ill.: Scripture Press Ministries, 1978), p. 14.

[2]Andrew Greeley, *Love and Play* (Chicago: The Thomas More Press, 1975), p. 64.

CHAPTER SIX

THE RECEPTION AFTER THE RECEPTION
LEARNING TO LISTEN CARINGLY

T he stars do seem to be closer, bigger, and brighter when you're in Texas. For that reason alone the spring and summer evenings we had there created some good memories for Ginger and me. One evening was unforgettable without even taking those brilliant lights of the sky into account, however. As we sat talking on the front lawn of our house, Ginger surprised me by interrupting the flow of our conversation. "Chick, Chick," she said loudly. Startled, my eyes automatically shifted from the stars to her face. "What's wrong?" I asked. "You're listening to me," she said. "Yes, you're really listening to me."

I may not have realized it then, but that turn of my head signaled a turn in our marriage. For me, communication breakdown occurs less in my sending set than in my reception apparatus. The fact that Ginger made her remark after seven years of marriage shows just how severe my listening problem was.

Listening to Understand

To my comfort, Paul Tournier claims that most people, like me, are poor listeners. He says: "Each one speaks primarily in order to set forth his own ideas. . . . Exceedingly few exchanges of viewpoints manifest a real desire to understand the other person."[1]

Moreover, it takes *two* good listeners to make one good marriage. Research which compared twelve troubled marriages with twelve non-troubled marriages makes this clear. Couples in troubled relationships more often misunderstood one another and more often felt misunderstood. What most astonished the researchers was the fact that they could not correctly identify the specific issue on which misunderstanding existed.[2] In other words, it was not the many misunderstandings that plagued the researchers; it was the misunderstanding. Most troubled couples are not as incompatible as they are incommunicado.

This is true because understanding is so central to a satisfying relationship. When we are understood we feel loved. Judson Swihart says it so well: "Virtually every time a person feels understood, feels that his spouse understands his emotional needs, he will also feel loved."[3]

Lapsing into Misunderstanding

Being misunderstood feels as bad as being understood feels good. It hurts whenever your partner either distorts your message or doesn't want to receive it.

One wife explains: "I only wish my husband would respond to me." Her husband Tom did not know what to do with Sandy's emotional needs. So he just froze up and ignored them. When she expressed her feelings, Tom didn't comment. His lack of involvement meant, "I don't know how to help you," but she heard, "I don't care that you are hurting." Of course that meant, "I don't care about you." It was difficult for Sandy because now, in addition to her hurt, she was also trying to deal with her feelings about what she thought was Tom's lack of caring.[4]

Since understanding is associated with love, misunderstanding amounts to rejection. And that's tragic. "The loneliest people in the world," according to one communication expert, "are usually people who are frequently misunderstood. To be stuck with thoughts, feelings, and intentions that no one really knows about is an awful place to be stuck."[5]

That may also be the basic reason why the Apostle Peter's first word to husbands is *"live with your wives in an understanding way"* (1 Peter 3:7 NASB). James, too, stresses its importance. *"Everyone should be quick to listen, slow to speak and slow to become angry"* (1:19). Failure to understand is downright foolishness, according to the wisdom of Proverbs. *"A fool finds no pleasure in understanding but delights in airing his own opinions"* (18:2). In the Old Testament a fool is not only stupid; he is sinful.

Our sinful human nature thrives on misunderstanding. God makes it clear that conflict and rejection of one another is deeply rooted in our selfishness (cf. James 4:1, 2.) Trying hard to enter into the thoughts and feelings of another is a very unselfish act.

The Apostle Paul urged Christians to *"accept one another, then, just as Christ accepted you"* (Romans 15:7). The Greek word translated "accept" is the same one used to refer to people taking food at a banquet. I can't think of anything that would produce a more fantastic marriage than if two people were to reach out for each other's thoughts and feelings as eagerly as they reach for a slice of their favorite pie. Praying the prayer of St. Francis will help: "That I seek to understand rather than to be understood."

Tuned Out: Left Out

Seeing the nature of misunderstanding will underscore its importance. Misunderstanding is far more than just not hearing. We can learn to accept certain frequent communication blackouts. When the cookies are chunks of charcoal because a husband fails to turn off the oven at 4:00, he says, "I forgot." Most often, he just failed to hear his wife's instructions in the first place. At some point the communication loss begins to have more serious consequences than burned bakeries, though.

Isolating by Not Hearing

Misunderstanding becomes serious when one partner regularly fails to heed the other's plea to be understood. In the evening, a wife says, "I really felt rather down today." The husband responds: "I wonder if the football game will be on TV tonight." Though in the same room, she is left isolated, and wonders why.

An insensitive listener makes it very difficult for his partner to share the very intimate. Summoning courage, a husband dares to signal his anxiety about getting close to thirty. He says, "We celebrated the birthday of one of the guys at work today. He's twenty-seven. I'll be twenty-nine soon; sounds awfully old to me."

Unaware of what is happening, his wife says, "I think it's nice you have those little celebrations at work." She didn't hear. She heard the word "birthday," but not the message of the words "awfully old." She failed to tune in at a time when he needed her. It took courage to say what he did; now he feels too foolish about his anxieties to share his thoughts again. He drops the subject. He feels alone. She didn't see the open doorway to his heart.

Rejecting by Rubber Stamping

Rejection can take a form much more negative than not hearing or mis-hearing. We are especially unkind when we judge instead of trying first to understand.

A wife wants to talk about her confusion over values. She asks herself about the amount of money she should spend on clothes in light of the needs of the world. Hoping to discuss this she says to her husband, "I have been rethinking our decision to buy that expensive dress." His reply is abrupt and thoughtless: "I think you should buy it." If she contradicts him, they may end up arguing. So she backs off.

How much better if he had first said, "Why are you rethinking it?" Then, he would have opened his mind to hers; he would have become a sounding board, a friend who would help her think through and sort out her thoughts on a difficult issue of life. Instead he became the judge behind the bench, banging his gavel, making his judgment.

We all seem to have this tendency to want to play the part of "his honor." Something inside of us makes us want to approve or disapprove of what someone says. We feel responsible if we let a statement go by unappraised. I call this feeling, "the anxiety of the rubber stamp."

Whenever anyone says something, we feel compelled to bang our mark on it: "I agree," or "I disagree." The stamp our partners are looking for, first of all, is the one that says: "I understand." Then, of course, we can offer our opinion. But giving an opinion is rarely a good substitute for giving a listen.

Hurting by Missing the Feeling

When we judge too soon, we not only close the conversation, we can inflict hurt we didn't intend to. A lot of episodes like the following can lead to friction between a couple.

He says, "I'm really worried about finishing that project by next Friday." She snaps back, "You shouldn't worry; Christians are not supposed to be anxious." Talking with her is about as comforting as explaining to the traffic cop why you didn't see the 35 mph speed limit sign. Part of this misunderstanding is due to the choice of words. Once he said the term "worried," she thought immediately of sin. Had he used the word "concerned," she might have responded differently. Yet the fault was hers. First of all she needed to find out what her husband meant by his statement.

This example also illustrates another way people are made to feel misunderstood. It has little to do with words. Instead it centers on the feelings behind them. In the previous exampl⸱ a wise listener would have asked herself, "Why is my husband mentioning his worry?" It should have been quite obvious he was trying to tell her about his inner anxiety. He was looking for support and encouragement. What she needed to respond to were his feelings, not his words. Later in the chapter, I will offer you some practice at doing this.

Misinterpreting the feelings that accompany the words can be as bad or worse than missing it. For example, the following statement has no doubt started a lot of quarrels: "I really don't feel like going to the party tonight." If the listener responds to the wrong emotion, neither will feel like a party. If a wife judges that he doesn't feel like being with her, she could accuse, "You never feel like being with me." Suppose, to the contrary, the husband had made the statement because he had just the opposite feelings. The rascal had in mind a private party just for the two of them.

A number of these kinds of misunderstandings may not destroy a relationship. When they occur often and at crucial times, they can hurt, though. Some occasions are more sensitive than others. In regard to her husband's economic setback, a wife says, "I really feel discouraged because you lost that contract." Taking it to mean she is angry with him, he replies sarcastically, "Sure, I deliberately went right down there to blow it, didn't I?" In such cases, not understanding equals misunderstanding. And being misunderstood makes us feel uncared for and unloved.

Tuning In

The many facets of misunderstanding show us how complicated understanding each other can be. Communication's greatest illusion may be that it is easily achieved. Living in the same house hour after hour will not automatically breed understanding.

Handling the Habits

We will have to work at it, to change the non-listening habits we developed as we grew up. We don't give people a chance to talk. We fidget with things, conveying an attitude of nervousness or disinterest. We don't stop, and look, and listen.

We keep changing the subject and rephrasing what people are saying, making them feel foolish. We interrupt. We finish our partner's sentences because we smugly think we have him or her figured out. We insert funny remarks whenever someone is trying to be serious. Such well developed, destructive habits won't be changed overnight. Patience and effort are musts for change.

Most of all, you will both have to value a dependent relationship. If either of you has learned to live comfortably alone with his thoughts and feelings, you may not care whether you understand or are understood. This makes life tough for your partner. When one of you wants to be understood but the other doesn't want to understand, further misunderstanding is created.[6] Therefore, you first need to talk about talking . . . and listening.

The following discussion not only offers some good guidelines for listening, but you can use it as a springboard for a discussion about how well you are understanding each other.

These suggestions are based on the idea that good listening involves each partner . . . totally. Understanding involves more than having a good set of ears.

Listen with Your Mind

Good listening is, at its core, thoughtful concentration, especially about two things: What is your partner thinking, and what is he or she feeling. Let's focus on how to listen for what your partner is thinking.

Sometimes the words your partner uses mean different things to you. If she says, "I think that woman is mean," you better find out what she has in mind when she says "mean" before you respond. If he says, "I am really troubled," you will need more data before you can understand.

One very effective way for getting an accurate picture of the person's thoughts is to ask questions. Concentrate on those that start with what, when, where, or how.

Taking one of the previous examples, we can see how good questions might have avoided a misinterpretation. Wife: "I have been rethinking our decision to buy that expensive dress." Husband: "What do you mean by rethinking? Have you changed your mind?" Wife: "No, I just haven't finally decided." Husband: "What is making you rethink it?" Wife: "I was reading the other day about the need for Bible schools to train new African Christians, and it made me feel like we could be able to give more to missions." Husband: "You think that buying that dress is preventing us from giving more?" Wife: "Yes, that's what I have been thinking. What do you think?"

Now the couple is into a discussion that could lead to some changes in their lives. It will at least give the wife a chance to examine her own thinking.

Another excellent way to make certain you understand another's thoughts is to simply restate the words in your words; paraphrase them. It's a simple device, but it does take practice to get used to doing it.

When the husband said, "I'm really worried about finishing the project by next Friday," the wife could have tried paraphrasing his statement. "You mean, you are seriously concerned about whether or not you have the time to get it done?" This is bound to make him feel accepted, despite his anxiety. He will be glad to continue to talk it out with her.

If you want to be an understanding person, you will not merely need to learn to listen for the meaning of the words. You will also need to train yourself to tune into the feeling behind the words. Husbands may especially need to work at doing this. This is because women may use speech differently than men. Paul Tournier makes note of this difference.

> Speech itself has a different meaning for men than it has for women. Through speech men express ideas and communicate information. Women speak in order to express feelings, emotions. This explains why a wife will relate ten times an experience she has lived. It is not to inform her husband. He cuts her off sharply, "I know it already; you've told it to me before." But she needs to tell it again in order to discharge emotional tension which the experience has built up in her heart.[7]

We need not agree with Tournier to benefit from his statement. Whether women use words to express feelings more than do men is not our main focus. The important fact to be noted is that all of us do this. When we do, it is critical that someone we love seeks to understand us and helps us with our emotional needs.

Sometimes we can easily detect our partner's emotional state from his words. The statement "I feel lousy about losing that sale," is an obvious attempt to get the bad feelings off the chest.

However, emotions sometimes hide behind the words and are not so easily spotted. If she says, "I should have bought those shoes," she may not be asking for a discussion about the clothes budget. Sensitive to this, a husband might say, "You really feel badly about the decision you made, don't you?" This gives her a chance to share her discouragement and get help to work through it.

Deliberate practice will make you more efficient at spotting emotions. Once you see the feelings, you can make a more appropriate response. See what feelings you can find behind the following statements. Compare your answers with those that follow. Then you fill in the responses appropriate to your own particular situation.

He Says:	He Might Be Feeling	Response He Might Need From Me
1. Did you see how clean her house was? She sure is well organized.		
2. You don't seem to offer me the support you used to.		
3. Shall I watch the kids while you get a little rest for awhile.		
4. How come you have to spend all evening sewing that dress?		
5. Boy! I have to give two speeches next month.		

The Reception After the Reception

She Says:	She Might Be Feeling	Response She Might Need From Me
1. You rarely say nice things like that. 2. I wish you would rub the back of my neck for just a minute. 3. I just can't manage Jeff when he gets like that. 4. You did such a good job on that report; can I make a special snack for you? 5. Your secretary said you guys were having a blast on that project; sounded a lot more exciting than cleaning this house.		

Answers:

He Might Be Feeling	She Might Be Feeling
1. Resentful, frustrated	1. Neglected, frustrated
2. Inadequate, neglected, anxious	2. Lonely, neglected, affectionate
3. Understanding, sympathy	3. Helpless, frustrated, resentful, inadequate
4. Neglected, unloved, lonely, jealous	4. Proud, understanding, satisfaction
5. Anxious, pressured	5. Resentful, left out, alone, bored, sorry for self

Listen with Your Posture

When people were asked to tell what poor listening habits in others irritated them most, they included the following:

> He continually fidgets with a pencil, a paper, or something, looking at it and examining it as if studying it . . . rather than listening to me.

> He twitches and turns constantly, just waiting for me to stop so he can take over.

> He doesn't put down what he is doing when I come in and turn his attention to me completely.

All of these complaints have to do with listening posture. A person may be listening. But he doesn't look like he is. And the person who is talking feels neglected and hurt.

This is one of the most common complaints of husbands and wives: "He/she just won't stop and look to listen." To overcome this, married people will have to determine that listening is too important not to drop things and concentrate. They will make certain their body language is saying to the talker: "I'm interested; I'm hearing you; I want to understand." This is usually done by sitting still, looking at the talker, bending forward, nodding, and making other nonverbal motions to communicate a positive response.

Many individuals are not even conscious about how indifferent they look.

A pastor was shocked into awareness at one of the seminars I was conducting. After the participants had used a checklist to evaluate themselves as listeners, he sat there resting his chin on the palm of his hand with a look of astonishment. "What's wrong?" I asked. He shook his head in dismay over his own blindness. An item on the list, he said, had made him see himself. His wife had continually accused him of not listening to her. Considering himself to be a good listener, he never understood her complaint. Now he did.

It was the way he treated her when she came to talk to him. When anyone would come into his study, he would drop what he was doing and concentrate on what they were saying. But whenever his wife popped in, he continued to glance at the mail or write, thinking he could keep on doing his work and listen to his wife at the same time. He now knew his posture was telling the one he cared the most about . . . he hardly cared for at all.

Since we must listen with our whole body, then, listening is quite an active process. It includes more than absorbing sound like acoustical ceiling tile. Listening involves responding, nonverbally and verbally. Cultivating good verbal responses is what we'll concentrate on next.

Listen with Your Mouth

Whenever someone shares a thought or a feeling with us, there are a surprising number of responses we could give. Some of the initial responses are so negative that they can set the tone for the whole day or even the whole marriage.

One damaging response consists of trying to change the person's feelings. "Don't feel that way," we say to someone who has just told about his feeling of sadness. We somehow assume that the feelings, like demons, can be cast out by a few words. Our depressed partner has probably been telling himself the same thing all day long. He or she is not looking for a command, but for compassion. Empathy and understanding combine to make good treatment for negative emotions. Perhaps there are times when someone needs a scolding and a command, but not without first receiving understanding.

Blame and thoughtless orders are never proper substitutes for understanding. Most of us need to hear, "Tell me how you feel," rather than, "You shouldn't feel that way."

Another improper response stems from reacting to our own feelings instead of our partner's statement. This happens simply because our partner's emotional state and statements have a way of arousing intense feelings in us. We end up concentrating on them instead of hearing out our husband or wife.

Think of what might happen when the husband greets his wife with, "I don't feel like going to a party." Perhaps she has been having some of these same feelings and fighting them all day, because she knows they need more social life. His statement acts like a glass of ice water on a warm back. It drenches what feeling she had for going out as well as angers her.

She responds, head down, walking out of the room, half shouting, "Now, I don't feel like going, either." He feels blamed and misunderstood. He could have been seeking some help from her. But because his statement aroused her emotions, he got a response based on her feelings . . . not his.

This kind of reply can be especially troubling when a couple is responding to some stress. If a wife is ill and depressed, she may look for consolation by saying, "I really feel discouraged over being sick for so many days." Discouraged himself, her husband may fail to be helpful to her: "How do you think I feel?" he says, drawing attention to himself.

If you become aware of various kinds of responses, you'll soon get into the habit of saying the right thing at the right time. *"How good is a timely word,"* Proverbs 15:23 tells us.

Timely responses come in many forms.

Interpreting. First of all there is the "Here's what you mean" reaction. In this case, the listener tries to help the other person interpret what he is thinking and feeling. The reply looks something like this: "Sounds to me like you are more angry with yourself than with him." This answer makes the listener appear as a friend, not as a judge.

Exploring. Another helpful type of answer is the "Let's dig deeper" statement. This shows your partner that you intend to help him/her seek more information and explore further what they have said. This type will sound like this: "Is there any evidence that what you say is happening is really the case?" "Have you felt like this before and what did you do about it then?" By this the listener is saying "Let me help you stop, think about it, and figure it out."

Understanding. The "I think this is what you mean" response is always in order. This reply shows the talker that the listener, above all, wants to understand him. This can be done by restating or paraphrasing that which was described earlier.

Supporting. Another category of great answers could be called the "I am with you" type. These statements say to the speaker "I understand what you are saying and I want to reassure you your reaction is normal, your thinking is O.K." In effect, you are moving in to lend your support, hoping that the person will lose some of the intensity of feeling within the accepting atmosphere you are creating. When you respond in this way you are not so much speaking to the issue as you are trying to encourage the person. You say things like: "I've felt that way." "I hear you." "Go ahead, say how you feel; it will help."

Judging. This final category of response is different from the others. The previous statements all reflect on what the speaker is thinking. Avoiding any judgment, they only help the speaker expand, explore, accept, and understand what he is saying. Sometimes your partner will want more than this. He/she will want to know your opinion. The "Here's what I think" answer is sometimes timely. This includes a judgment and evaluation of what the person has said. You offer your point of view without a critical spirit.

To clarify in your mind the exact description of these responses, try labeling each of the following responses to this statement: "I can't help it, but I really get angry over my mother's meddling. She still seems to want to control my life and I can't make her see how upset her interference makes me feel."

Responses: (Possible answers are: Interpreting, Exploring, Understanding, Supporting, Judging)

"What especially bothers you about the way she acts?"

"I can't blame you for getting upset. I think she is out of bounds and you should do something about it."

"You mean that you get disturbed because she doesn't seem to trust your ability to handle things?"

"You seem to feel you have not really broken loose from her and that her attempts to help are really attempts to control you."

"I have felt the same way about my parents. I think it is only natural to feel this way—especially since you are in a sort of transition period."

Check your answers with these to determine your grasp of these responses. They are (E), (J), (U), (I), (S).

Now ask yourself, Which of these are my most common responses? Any of these responses could be good, depending on the situation. However, if you are always making judging and interpreting comments, your partner may not get a chance to explain himself as fully as when you respond in other ways. Your partner will get the impression that you are always judging and never really trying to understand. *Good* responses will be positive ones that seek understanding.

In contemporary circles today, there is an unusual emphasis on listening. Sometimes it is not for the right reason. As one super salesman said, "Put yourself in the other fellow's shirt so that he'll take it off and give it to you." In other words, we can use our understanding to manipulate other people for our own advantage.

Our motive for understanding should be based on what our

spouse gains from it and on what it does for our marriage. Understanding each other is one of the most rewarding experiences of the intimate relationship. If you work at it, your spouse will love you for it. Won't it be great to be able to say of one another: "Above all else, my partner understands me."

Commune Occasion

Improving Our Listening Skills:

First, choose from the following list of listening problems the ones your spouse does not have. Share these in affirmation of each other.

1. Failing to hear instructions like: "Turn off the oven at 4:00."
2. Failing to hear subtle statements about anxiety or other feelings my partner wants to discuss.
3. Rejecting statements by giving negative judgments.
4. Rejecting statements by always taking the other side.
5. Rejecting statements by changing the subject.
6. Missing a chance to listen by giving reasons why I agree.
7. Failing to understand whenever my partner is trying to share a feeling by his or her statement.
8. Failing to understand what feeling is behind the statement.
9. Misinterpreting a feeling behind a statement that is made.
10. Reacting based on my own feeling generated by the other's statement.
11. Not stopping what I am doing and showing a listening posture.
12. Constantly interrupting.
13. Finishing my partner's statement.
14. Thinking I know what my partner is saying or going to say and thus misunderstanding.
15. Failing to understand what is said by asking questions before responding.
16. Never attempting to paraphrase a statement in order to show I understand.
17. Tending to tell the partner not to feel the way he does.
18. Failing to use many types of responses, such as interpreting,

exploring, understanding, supporting, and judging—but always responding with the same type.

Next go over the above list to choose those listening problems that you believe you yourself have. Do not evaluate your partner but evaluate yourself. Then share these with your partner and see if he/she agrees with your evaluation. You may then share what problems you do see in your partner and discuss ways of improving your understanding.

ENDNOTES

[1]Paul Tournier, *To Understand Each Other,* trans. John S. Gilmour (Atlanta, Ga.: John Knox Press, 1967), p. 4.

[2]R. D. Laing, H. Phillipson, and A. R. Lee, *Interpersonal Perception: A Theory and Method of Research,* p. 86, quoted in Sherod Miller, Elam E. Nunnally, Daniel B. Wackman, *Alive and Aware* (Minneapolis: Interpersonal Communications Programs, Inc., 1976), p. 149.

[3]Judson J. Swihart, *How Do You Say, "I Love You,"* (Downers Grove, Ill.: Inter-Varsity Press, 1977), p. 43.

[4]Ibid..

[5]Miller, Nunnally, Wackman, *Alive and Aware,* p. 148.

[6]Ibid., p. 127.

[7]Tournier, *To Understand Each Other,* p. 40.

CHAPTER SEVEN

MAKING SENSE OF THE SENSUAL
THE BIBLICAL PURPOSE OF SEX IN MARRIAGE PART 1

R ecently some mountain climbers gained nationwide attention by scaling Mt. Rainier. The world noticed them because they were not ordinary climbers. All but their leader were handicapped: five blind, two deaf, an epileptic, and one with an artificial leg.

As the conquered mountain was capped with snow, their feat was capped with special significance. Not only did they enjoy the fun and excitement of ascending a towering Cascade peak; they experienced the meaning of that accomplishment. They were out to prove something to themselves and others. The real impact was in what the climb meant—not in the climb itself.

Sex is like that. Included in the experience is all the fun, novelty, exhilaration, and excitement of a mountain climb. Still, the lasting flavor is in its meaning. Most of us do not want just sex; we long for what it means.

Seeing Beyond the Physical

That is why good sex technique is not all that is needed in the marital bed. A couple can know how to get the maximum physical pleasure out of sex, but eventually get bored with one another. This is because sex is more than a sensual linking of bodies; it is a joining of two persons. What that encounter means to those two individuals is what counts most of all.

Lack of meaning also makes people uncomfortable with sex. A man once told me that even after twenty years of marriage, his wife was having trouble enjoying sex, thinking of it as a mere animal act. This tendency to view sex as only physical may be what makes many moderns so uptight about it. "Sexperts" Masters and Johnson claim that more than half of married couples surveyed have major problems in this area of their marriage.

When we see beyond the physical, it will help us cultivate a positive attitude toward this gift of God. A pastor in one of my courses recently reported what was occurring in his marriage. "After my wife and I read that good book on sex, I could later see her loosening up in our sexual episodes," he wrote. She was able to enjoy and participate in the physical aspects of her marriage once she was more aware of its broader meaning.

What is true for her seems true of others. A *Redbook* survey revealed that religious women enjoyed sex in marriage more than nonreligious women did. The authors of the report explained religious women more readily accepted their bodies and their sexual activities as something created by God. Thus they were able to comprehend more fully the meaning of this side of marriage.

Because this meaning is so crucial, this chapter and the next will unfold the biblical purposes of sex. The practical suggestions will then flow out of this survey of God's purpose for sex in marriage.

Sex Offers Us a Part in God's Creating

In the opening pages of the book of Genesis, human sexuality is linked with human reproduction. *"God created man in his own image . . . male and female he created them. God blessed them and said to them, 'Be fruitful and increase in number; fill the earth and subdue it' "* (Genesis 1:27, 28). This statement includes God's first order to man. And, with the vast world population today, we can at least say that mankind has obeyed the first commandment.

Though it's quite obvious that one of the purposes of sex is reproduction, what this implies is not so obvious.

The Image of God and the Image of Sex

God chose sexual intercourse to produce persons in His image.

Consequently, what great respect for sex we should have! As Billy Graham once said to a beach full of college kids, "Sex is all right; without it none of us would be here."

The biological function in sex should in no way cause a shameful downgrading of it. The Apostle Paul blamed the irreverence for marriage and sex on false teachers. In fact, he traced it to their following *"deceiving spirits and things taught by demons"* (1 Timothy 4:1). Such persons *"forbid people to marry . . . which God created. . . ."* He then reminds us *"everything God created is good"* (4:3).

Christian couples should have a high regard for their sex life. And if and when their sensual activity gives birth to a child, it should make them even more appreciative of each other's bodies. As they grow old together, stretch marks should provoke admiration, not disgust. Because their male and female bodies have brought adored children into the world, those bodies should be more cherished in each other's eyes.

Not Being Indifferent to Difference

We should respect the different roles played by the man and the woman in sex since intercourse can lead to the birth of a baby. And we should consider what difference the distinctive roles make in each partner's attitude toward sex. Playing a different part will surely color the way each looks at sex. As someone has said, "For a man, sexual intercourse could last for nine minutes; for a woman, it could last nine months."

Because the female bears the child in her body, she has tended to be more cautious about a sexual relationship. She approaches it in a more total way, wanting some security in the relationship for the future security of the potential child. There is evidence for this attitude today in the fact that most women will only justify sexual intercourse outside of marriage if they are "in love."

Contraceptives may be changing all of this. More women are grabbing the freedom to have nonmarital sex, an indicator of a change in attitude. They may be becoming as casual about it all as men have sometimes been.

Yet some believe the differences linger because they are caused by more than culture, being natural to the sexes. Even those who think differences in sexual attitude are outdated admit to their existence. For example, social scientist Catherine Hahner says:

"Women are stuck with an obsolescent desire to feather their nest, furnish the cage, while men grow progressively less interested." She then admits: "This sounds sexist, but I'm convinced that women have a psychic predisposition toward monogamy, evolved through hundreds of thousands of years of responsibility for the survival of their offspring and dependence on a male provider."[1]

Understanding the difference between you does not mean condoning extramarital sex for either of you. Both men and women were created to be loyal to each other in their marriage. Men may experience the temptation to stray more than women because of the different biological role they have played through the centuries. But stronger temptation can't be used as the rationale for straying behavior.

What the Differences Mean to You.   What this means primarily is that in your sexual experience you will need to take into account the distinctions between you. The man will need to understand his wife's concern for developing the total relationship, not just the erotic. A husband will need to work harder at developing the total relationship in order to have a good sex life with his partner. Not that she is incapable of enjoying the erotic. It's just that she tends to see sex in context. If it is with a husband who cares, who is committed, who is gentle and considerate, it will be more rewarding to her.

The wife will need to better grasp the man's perspective. He may be, especially in the early years of marriage, very caught up in the erotic, physical aspects of sex. Ellen Key said years ago: "With women love usually proceeds from the soul to the senses and sometimes does not reach so far . . . with man it usually proceeds from the senses to the soul and sometimes never completes the journey."

Most men's physical capacity for sex peaks at age eighteen, a bit of information which can make a wife recognize how unquenchable the sensual fire is within him. She will need to excuse him for sometimes forgetting the personal side to sex, and then help him cultivate a larger understanding of what it means.

In the meantime, she will need to cultivate her appetite for the physical sensation of sex. She knows that by the time she reaches her early thirties, her sexual passion will peak. She must not permit early attitudes and perspectives to interfere with the growing sexual harmony. There is lots of evidence that as couples approach their middle years together, they will be much more alike in their approach. The husband will have become more appreciative of the more spiritual, personal aspects of intimacy, while the wife will be more passionate about the physical.

What the Differences Mean in Your View of Others.   Not only does this distinction between male and female show up in the way you view sex with each other, it will affect the way you view other people. Psychologist James Dobson urges wives not to misunderstand and blame their husbands if they may not be too discriminating when it comes to what or who turns them on. The man is quite visually oriented. When he sees a beautifully shaped female or a picture of a scantily clad one, whether extremely beautiful to him or not, he thinks of sex. He becomes aroused even if he doesn't know anything about the IQ, personality, or background of the person occupying that body.

Women, who are more discriminating, have difficulty understanding this. While it is true that a woman may get excited by her husband's nude body, other factors are more influential. She first warms up to his tenderness, strength, courage, or compassion—then to his touch, and then to his body.

Thus, when a wife sees her husband's head turn as a perfumed, seductively dressed woman strolls by, she may misunderstand. She may feel he is more interested in others than in her. She may accuse him of not being satisfied with their marriage. In reality, he is probably not interested in others, nor dissatisfied; he is just a man. His mechanism is such that temptation comes first of all to him through the eyes. However, that may not mean he has sinned, since temptation is not equal to sin.

The woman, too, will be tempted. She will be caught feeling warm sensations when she sees an actor perform or a man give a speech (even a minister preaching a sermon). She is turned on by the man's strength or wisdom or his charm-filled vibrations.

What we do with these sights and impressions determines whether or not we have done wrong. A man who takes too many second looks and cultivates sexual thoughts may be near the sin of coveting. A man contemplating unfaithfulness is sinning. This is what Jesus meant when He said, *"Anyone who looks at a woman lustfully has already committed adultery with her in his heart"*

(Matthew 5:28). Jesus could not have meant that every glance is sin. Otherwise we would have to equate temptation and sin, which the Bible does not. Jesus, Himself, was tempted and yet without sin.

Jesus was referring to the intent to commit adultery; He was speaking of the husband who has already decided to seduce the one on whom he is looking. While most men may have looked at other women with thoughts of sex, it does not mean that they have done so with intentions. There is a major difference. Married men and women, catching themselves contemplating sex with someone other than their partner, must immediately prune the thought from their mind. Pondering such thoughts is dangerously close to making provision for the powerful lusts within us.

Looking, then, may be quite innocent and natural for a man. Since he may be caught looking at another female, it follows that he will enjoy looking at his wife's body. It seems that it is biologically built into him to be attracted by her feminine features. Being turned on so easily and so quickly, he is usually the sexual aggressor in his marriage. The woman, however, has means of aggression in her power. How she dresses or doesn't dress is a powerful ploy for her initiating a sexual encounter between them.

This discussion is not to tell you what should be the female or male place and attitude in sexual relationships. What is normal for you is whatever is natural for you. The Bible does not dictate who should be the aggressor or that males and females should view sex differently. This section is only meant to make you aware that differences may exist. And they will make a difference. Be alert.

On the Sixth Day, God Created Hormones

The procreative function of sex should remind us how very physical it is. Strange that we sometimes don't want to admit this.

In the past, Christian writers tended to equate sexual passion with animal-like behavior. But sensual, erotic passion in a human is human. Never have I found in the pages of Scripture the notion that men and woman can act like animals. Sadly, examples of animal-like attitudes exist. A friend of mine once confided that his wife had lost interest in sex and she wasn't willing any longer to satisfy his "animal passion." The erotic side of marriage should not be put down by making it less than human. When God created man and woman, he created the glands, hormones, nerves, impulses, and passions that should function unrestrained between a husband and wife.

If we ignore this physical side of sex, we may also fail to see how powerful it is. We may tend to think sex should be easy to control: to turn off and turn on as easily as our mind flips from one subject to another. Yet the sex drive is extremely physical and in part uncontrollable. There is an internal chemistry at work, triggered by stimuli picked up by the senses. Sometimes this inner gyrating dominates our thought life. It destroys our concentration even though we are trying to get involved in our day's work.

The Apostle Paul understood this. He urged people to get married rather than continue to burn with lust (1 Corinthians 7:9). He knew they couldn't silence their sexual mechanism, but that they could manage it.

Because sex is so physical, it means that we can't always easily control what happens to us; and we should especially remember that our partner can't either. A man may expect his partner to be ready for sex any time he desires without recognizing that there may be physical reasons for lack of interest. He may get annoyed with his wife even though fatigue or her menstrual cycle is robbing her of her desire for him.

A woman, too, may fail to comprehend how sexual arousal will affect her husband, making him irritable and unable to sleep, etc. There are physical reasons for this. Even his immediate response to the completion of the act of intercourse may cause her dismay: he rolls over and goes to sleep or gets up to make a sandwich instead of lingering in her arms while her passion slowly subsides.

On the one hand she needs to realize that when he climaxed, he emptied numerous glands throughout his body, leaving him relaxed and turning his mind immediately from sexual things. She needs to be patient with his after-coital activities. But on the other hand, he will try to recognize her need to be held while her body and emotions more slowly subside to their normal state.

Some Good Advice: Learn All You Can

Therefore, it makes sense for you to learn all you can about the physical aspects of sex. You will learn, as one expert explains, "Doing what comes naturally will fail every time." He is referring to the fact that a man's readiness time for sex is so much shorter than a woman's. A man is like a pile of dry leaves, easily ignited and arising to extreme heat quickly. A woman is physically more like a pile of charcoal; she is slow to get burning, but arrives at the same intensity of heat as the male. But it takes longer. Were a husband and wife to do what comes naturally, he would climax before she was even beginning to get some interest.

A good sex manual will help you understand these matters. You may even discover that you haven't fully learned about your own or your partner's sexual anatomy. Many men and women enter marriage with little understanding of the role of the woman's clitoris in sexual response. This is so small and inconspicuous in many women that they may hardly be aware of its existence. And unless men are told by their wives or informed from conversation or reading, they may not know the role of the clitoris in intercourse, particularly the part it plays in bringing on the woman's orgasm. This ignorance can cause trouble especially during those first few sensitive months of marriage.

Despite the obvious need for sex manuals, I have met Christians who objected to them. Books like these are a sensible way of communicating information today that may have more easily been communicated by parents or uncles in the past. If it makes sense to have books on how to garden, and how to take care of your parakeets, it makes sense to have a book or two on the complicated matter of how to relate sexually. Several excellent books are listed in the reading list at the end of this book.

Sex Offers Us Communion

Sex in marriage goes beyond the role of procreation as a study of Genesis, chapter 2, indicates. Whereas in Genesis, chapter 1, the emphasis falls on populating the earth, the emphasis in Genesis 2 is different. There sex is linked with companionship more than it is with conception. God created woman and the sexual experience so that man would not be alone. It is through the sensual that he becomes one with the woman.

Sex in marriage is for creating oneness. The intimacy experienced in the union of bodies and emotional responses in this act is unmatched in human experience. *"Love is as strong as death,"* says the Song of Songs, indicating how powerful the sensual bond can be (8:6). It is not merely that the sexual embrace is itself a union; rather, it is that the sexual union is a channel and symbol of the union. Studies of people's experience of sex show how true that is. Both men and women say things like: "Sex makes me feel close." "Sex assures me of the intimate attachment I have with another person." "I feel accepted when we have intercourse."

During the actual physical joining, the couple's oneness in other areas is being fused. It is as if the sexual connection is a channel through which flows their mutual feeling, appreciation, and understanding. The flowing back and forth is sensual, but also emotional, intellectual, spiritual—involving the total person. Sex is also a symbol: In their naked union the couple symbolizes the communion they desire in other areas of life.

Nonmarital Sex Is Like Playing with a Telephone

It is this lofty purpose of sex in marriage that makes sex outside of marriage so wrong. Sex apart from marriage is sex apart from relationship. Sex belongs to those who are committed to a life-long, one-flesh relationship. Anything less than this strips sex of its meaning. It is using a communication device when you have nothing to communicate. It is like a child playing with a telephone when he has nothing serious to say.

When one person has sex with another, they ought to be saying: "I want to be joined to you; I want to commune with you with all my being." The physical joining is only a part of the total bonding. To join physically without desiring to join totally robs sex of its meaning.

This total intimacy is what makes it impossible to share sexual oneness with more than one person. The communion is too deep, too demanding, to be spread around. Spread too thinly, it will lose its significance . . . and thus cease to be. True oneness with another cannot be intentionally partial; you can't have sex together while holding back part of yourselves without eventually making it mechanical and unfulfilling. Sexual relating outside of marriage is wrong—not because sex is bad, but because it is so good.

This separation of sex from its meaning has plagued mankind's history. People exploit and deceive each other to satisfy their sensual desires. They hardly realize that their basic thirst for intimacy cannot be quenched in this way. In fact, there is evidence that sex without commitment may lead to a greater sense of loneliness. And it will most certainly not lead to long-lasting sexual satisfaction.

Joan Garrity is a prominent illustration of this. Author of one of the most explicit sexual books ever published by a woman, she became famous for her sexual promiscuity. The book she authored is entitled *The Sensuous Woman*, and she became an instant millionaire by describing her sexual exploits for all to read. The book explained to women how to have sex with anyone, anywhere, any time, and any way. People in North America gobbled up fourteen million copies of the book, making its author the most widely known female advocate of sex outside of marriage in U.S. history.

What is not so widely known is what Joan Garrity is now doing and thinking. More than ten years since she wrote *The Sensuous Woman,* she is now married. She has been writing a book on golf and another on cooking. After years of practicing and promoting sex without relationships, she now says, "The best sex is with someone you love." After years of experimentation, she now says what the Bible affirms: Sex is for oneness and oneness really makes sex worthwhile.

If Sex Is Language, What Are You Saying?

The importance of oneness in sex makes it imperative that a couple work hard at developing their sensual and their total intimacy. Each contributes to the other. Good relating will make sex good. And satisfying sex will help you relate well.

Of course, a poor sexual experience may hinder the broader intimacy. Since sex is a language, you must look closely at what you are communicating. Through sex, we can make beautiful statements to each other without uttering a word. When we have a gentle, warm, caring physical encounter we send messages like: "I love you; I care for you; I enjoy being with you; I comfort you; I like revealing myself to you; I like all of you."

But if the sex between us is not good, the messages aren't positive. Instead, we nonverbally declare: "I don't care for you; I have a hard time being with you; I don't like you; I don't care for all of you; I think you are strange; I don't like revealing myself to you."

Persons with inhibited partners will need to be patient. They will realize that a partner is not meaning to say some of the things that are communicated through the lack of sexual interest or response. A young wife presently unable to be comfortably undressed with her husband may be saying: "I don't like revealing myself to you." In reality, however, it may be that she can't reveal herself at all. The husband will need to understand and resist the tendency to interpret her actions in a negative way.

The spouse who has the inhibition will need to be aware of the possible messages that are being sent and try to make up for them. He or she will need to try very hard to explain what is happening. The inner struggle will need to be brought out into the open. The spouse will have to communicate in other ways the message he or she is not saying in bed.

For instance, a man who has a low sex drive, and tends to forget about his wife's needs, may unknowingly be saying he really doesn't care about her. He will need to realize this problem and begin to handle it. He should seek to develop his sexual interest in her on the one hand, while demonstrating his care for her in ways that she sees as meaningful. It is essential that a couple does not allow the bad messages sent during the early years of sexual adjustment to hinder the enrichment of their sexual and marital journey.

Don't Ignore the Negative Messages

These negative messages can be so strong in the offended partner's mind that their impact may not be fully understood by the one who is sending them. This accounts for how some marriages can deteriorate in such a short time. The following example is all too common.

Having dated for over two years, Frank and Louise are happy in the relationship after testing it, analyzing it, and thoroughly enjoying it for more than twenty-four months. So satisfied are they of the genuine respect, love, and understanding that exists between them, they decide to marry. The day before the wedding, when he says, "I love you," she fully believes him . . . as he does her.

But the honeymoon is a disappointment. Not only does it rain every day at a resort that doesn't live up to its brochures, but she discovers he is clumsy in bed. Whereas before he was considerate and romantic, now he is in a hurry and nervous. The novelty of the act and the joy of being alone with her makes it easy to satisfy his needs. But she doesn't climax once during the seven nights of lovemaking sessions.

In short, she feels disappointed, nervous, and unfulfilled. The problem probably lies both in his ignorance and in her unwillingness to tell him of her need. She pretends all is well because she doesn't want to hurt him.

As he continues to ignore her need, the bad feelings begin. Without words, he keeps saying to her: "I'm selfish; I don't care about you." But this could hardly be true. After two years of a tested, close relationship, will a man change so dramatically? She tries to convince herself this is not true.

The sexual problem continues to color their relationship blue and neither of them knows how to handle it. To keep their relationship positive, they will both need to talk a lot and overcome their ignorance and fears related to sex.

The messages of the marital bedroom are just too loud to ignore. Sex is a beautiful language. It's worth the trouble to learn how to speak it fluently.

Commune Occasion

Differing about Differences

Do you really believe that men and women approach sex differently? If so, how do these differences make a difference in marriage? This "Commune Occasion" will give you a chance to become more aware of how you each think and feel about this matter. It should help you understand and respect each other a great deal more.

Remember, as in other "Commune Occasions," you will need to be honest in sharing and very accepting in your listening.

Step One:

Each of you check whether or not you believe the following differences exist. (Note: All of the following are not necessarily established as true through research; they are given to prompt your thinking.)

YES   NO   Men are more turned on by what they see than women.

Women want sexual experiences less than men.

Making Sense of the Sensual

Women are more concerned about security in a relationship as a context for sex than are men.

Men want love to get sex; women want sex to get love.

Women appreciate the feeling of closeness they get through sex more than men do.

Men have a physical need for sexual release every few days that women do not have.

Women are more interested in petting before intercourse than are men.

The sensation of orgasm is very different for men and women.

Women can talk about sex easier than men.

Women tend to talk more during sex than do men.

Early in marriage women tend to feel more ashamed and embarrassed about sex than do men.

Women tend to be more romantic than men.

Other _____

Other _____

Step Two:

Starting with the first item on the list, share together your answer. Then discuss how each of you personally relates to your answer. Do you believe that the difference exists between the two of you? Permit the discussion to go into areas that will help you better understand each other and your approach to sex.

ENDNOTES
[1]Catherine Hahner, "Sex as Athletics," *Saturday Review,* May 1973, p. 66, Used by permission.

CHAPTER EIGHT

MAKING SURE OF THE SENSUAL
THE BIBLICAL PURPOSE OF SEX IN MARRIAGE PART 2

A TV spot announcement advertising a Tuesday Night at the Movies shows a close-up of a sensual, feisty female. In a slow staccato cadence, she voices her fiery challenge to the man standing before her: "I am more of a woman than you can handle." The picture fades and dramatic music rises, leaving the viewer to determine exactly what she meant.

Obviously, the statement and the scene were designed to conjure up fantasies related to physical sex. If the actress had said, "I am more of a person than you can handle," the effect would have been entirely different.

Thinking of a woman—or a man—only in terms of their sexual functioning is one of the damaging images our sensual society throws at us. Being a sex object is demeaning and depersonalizing. It focuses on the part as equivalent to the whole. To be a woman or a man is to be far more than a person who can function well sexually.

On the other hand, we should not lose sight of the sexual part of our personhood. Tied up with our identity as persons is the fact that we are one sex or the other. Acceptance of one's male or femaleness is part of what it means to be mated. God destined us to be one sex or the other. Jesus questioned, *"Haven't you read that at the beginning the Creator 'made them male and female'?"* (Matthew 19:4)

Sex Confirms Our Identity

Our self-identity as either male or female is not merely a temporary arrangement to facilitate reproduction. We have noted earlier that the male-female nature of man is tied up with the nature of God. It is even quite possible that the sexual distinction will continue into eternity. While Jesus said that there would not be marriage in heaven, He did not rule out the fact that we would still be identified as male or female. Though Paul says that we are all one in Christ Jesus, be we Jew, Greek, slave, free, male, female, we may still be known for such distinctions in the eternal future as a demonstration of oneness despite diversity.

And so whenever two married people experience sexual coupling, they are also confirming their image of themselves as either male or female. This is not to say that our male or femaleness is our most important image. The most significant idea about ourselves is that we are each children of God. This is why it is possible to have a healthy, whole self-concept as a single person.

But when a person is married, the feeling he has about himself will be related to the sexual side of marriage. For this reason, an impotent married man, unable for some reason to have intercourse, suffers a crisis of personhood. The woman who cannot have an orgasm or is unable to enjoy sexual intercourse is not merely missing out on some pleasure. She may feel an incompleteness in regard to what she thinks of herself.

Granted, such a person can compensate for the missing piece of the identity puzzle. Not every married couple must have a sizzling, athletic sexual expression to feel complete as individuals or as a couple. The actual physical sex is only part of the picture. In the area of sex, especially, couples should not try to keep up with the Joneses or the national average. What is most important is mutual satisfaction and fulfillment.

It is still true, however, that whenever there are problems of sexual expression or relational problems that prevent an appropriate sexual experience, an image problem will exist. The husband will be saying to himself, for example, "I don't feel like a man." Whereas in a good sexual relationship each will say, "You make me feel like a woman," or "You make me feel like a man."

Some very practical, exciting guidelines come into focus when you realize that God's Word ties sex in marriage to one's personal self-image.

Bravo! You're the Opposite Sex

First, the relationship between marital sex and self-image suggests we should affirm a partner for the sexual nature God has given to him or her. It isn't surprising that so much of lovemaking talk consists of positive statements about the loved one's maleness or femaleness.

The Song of Songs, like other love songs, explores the beauties of the man and the woman. Of her he says, *"How beautiful you are, my darling! Oh, how beautiful!"* (4:1). Then he proceeds to describe her very feminine charms, beginning with her eyes, moving down to her breasts. In chapter 7, his eyes wander from her feet to the flowing locks of her head. The picturesque phrases leave no doubt he sees her as a woman: *"Your graceful legs are like jewels . . . Your breasts are like two fawns . . . your neck is like an ivory tower . . . your hair is like royal tapestry."* (7:1b,3a,4a,5b).

But sexual affirmation is not something left to the man alone. In chapter 5 of the Song of Songs the woman also expresses her appreciation for his manly features: his body which is like polished ivory, arms that are rods of gold, a mouth that is full of sweetness, legs as pillars of marble. *"His mouth is sweetness itself; he is altogether lovely,"* she concludes.

A good sex life thrives on affirmation. Positive sex play and sexual intercourse are sexual affirmation. Whenever through speech and other daily activities you confirm each other as being what you each distinctively are, you enhance your chances of having satisfying sex. The positive affirmation adds meaning to the physical activities and vice versa. The two are inseparably bound together.

Charlie Shedd counsels men to work hard at affirming their wives. Sometime, he says, write down thirty things you really admire about your wife. Then on the first day of the month when every chance comes, mention to her the first compliment you have written. Do the same with the second comment on the second day, etc. After one month, think up four new items you appreciate and offer her a new one every week. What Shedd suggests for the husbands is also a good practice for the wives. No matter what way you do it, keep the accent on the positive.

This also means avoiding the negative—especially comments that demean the other for his or her sexual identity. Bad jokes and sarcastic comments will not help your sex lives. If you put one another down in the living room, it will be easier to do so in the bedroom.

Remember, too, that when you need to reject one another's advances, offers, or suggestions in regard to sex, do it as softly as you can. When a husband is turned down, he may feel down not just for missing out on some moments of pleasure, but because his manhood is rejected. It's important to have a good understanding between you at such times . . . to be able to explain and not just make excuses. Even a comment that affirms can make the rejection less painful: "I just can't get with it tonight, but I know I won't be able to stay away from a man like you for long," eases him down.

Naturally a woman can also feel a similar rejection and the husband needs to learn how to handle these times carefully. If we take too casual an attitude toward sexual activity, dismissing these encounters as amusing little moments in one's life, we could easily miss the legitimately significant role sex plays in our partner's life. We won't completely comprehend how easy it is to deeply wound. We will unwittingly continue to hurt, without understanding the extent of the pain, making the partner seem foolish for taking it all so seriously.

If You're Married to a Violin, Be a Bow

Another practical message arising out of the connection of sex with self-image is this: Assert your own sexuality. A man makes a woman feel like one by being a man. Assertion of her femaleness makes him feel his masculinity, too. The complete, uninhibited expression of your sexual nature will affirm the other. Like a violin and a bow, the two of you go together. As a violin can't truly be itself without a bow, so one of you can't realize your full identity without the other.

Perhaps this is what makes the unconcerned, unresponsive partner situation so serious. A woman who merely endures the marital act, or a man who merely obliges his wife, is being kind, but not too affirming.

Learning what your partner likes in sex is an important part of sexual adjustment. When you assert yourself as that kind of man or woman, you confirm the other's picture of herself or himself. In saying this, I am not talking about proving your manhood or womanhood. The contemporary concept of being able to be a super performer sexually is not what I am emphasizing. I am talking about fulfilling our sexual role . . . not proving it. Willingness to improve your sexual experience will be done, not to impress each other, but to assist the other in feeling good about his or her sexual image.

As much as it is possible, it is important to assert your maleness or femaleness in your partner's terms—not in your terms. A husband who tries to be the kind of man the guys in the locker room admire may not get a good response from his wife. He may try to play the role of strength and mastery, while she wants him to be warm and tender.

The wife also may misunderstand his view of a woman. She may attempt to project the missionary circle's view of a woman, shared by her female friends. While he may want a wife who is serious and devoted to God, he may also want her to be sexy and funloving. There need not be any contradiction in the image: A man can be both strong and tender; a woman can be both godly and sensual.

What a Woman Wants

In general terms, research does help us know something of what men and women want of one another. These findings may not apply to you and your partner at all. It will be most beneficial if you can discuss your own concepts with each other. The research findings may stimulate your discussion.

In general women want a man who is romantic. Not that the physical pleasures are unimportant. By romance, she wants surprise and newness in her relationship. In her adolescence she was caught up in the excitement and anticipation of meeting new boys and through them learning new things about herself and life. Romance meant being admired, not merely for her body, but for herself. It meant being cared for, having someone go out of the way to notice and even pamper her a bit.

A woman cannot bask in those teenage fantasies and expectations all of her life. But she will be disappointed if her husband permits the excitement and surprise to go from their romantic relationship. She expects married life to be a romantic trip on the love boat, not a routine ride on the seven A.M. commuter train. If she suffers too much disillusionment, she may end up escaping in romantic novels and daydreams, trying to take flight from a brutally boring relationship.

That is not to say a husband can fill every day with wild romance. Daily work will sap both of their energies. Realistic crises and other problems will have to be faced. But men of all vocations, incomes, and situations have learned how to creatively keep their marriages alive with the elements of romance.

Most wives are not asking for a cruise every year across the world. They would welcome the salad bar of the Captain's Steak Joynt across town. A woman wants the exciting, adoring company of her husband—his attention fixed firmly on her.

In his practical commentary on the Song of Songs, Jody Dillow offers some terrific suggestions for being romantic. While a husband will want to devise romantic approaches and ventures tailored just for his wife, Dillow's ideas will prime your creative pump.

Phone her during the week and ask her out for one evening that weekend without telling her where you are taking her.

Give her an evening completely off. Clean up the kitchen.

Park in some secluded spot and kiss and talk for an evening.

Draw a bath for her after dinner. Put a scented candle in the bathroom; add bath oil to the bath; send her right there after dinner and you clean up the dishes.

Phone her from work to tell her you were thinking nice thoughts about her.

Write her a love letter and send it special delivery.

Plan for a surprise weekend. Make reservations; when the time comes have her pack her suitcase, but don't tell her where you are going. Make it some place romantic.

Give her an all-over body massage with scented lotion.

Replace her old negligee.[1]

Most of these romantic notions are based on the premise that women are usually less turned on sexually by what is more obviously sexual to a man. A man's nakedness will probably arouse her less than a man's gentleness. She will be aroused by being touched, this we know. But the first touches will have to be slight and in the right context. Reaching out for her forearm while you sit across from her in a dimly-lit restaurant will probably excite her more than your reach for her naked thigh when in bed.

And so marriage manuals that used to talk about fore-play now discuss fore-thought. For a woman, sexual intercourse begins in her head, not in her bed. What you say when you leave in the morning will have something to do with her readiness in the evening.

Men, become experts at developing situations which

communicate to her that you care, that you are excited by her, that you respect her, and that you want to be with her. These will go a long way toward meeting her sentimental and sexual needs. And they will serve as the prelude to some wonderful sexual encounters for both of you.

What a Man Wants

In general terms, we can say that what a man wants sexually in a woman is responsiveness. It has been said that, while a man wants a lady in the living room, he wants a mistress in the bedroom. This does not mean that he necessarily is looking to her to introduce variety in sexual technique. He usually will be the one to introduce the novel. He does want a wife who is interested in sex and who has a positive attitude about it. While she may be concerned that sex is satisfying and pleasant to him, he wants it to be for her as well.

Even a woman who at first associates sex with duty and dirtiness can improve her outlook on sex. Like other areas of life, sex is a learned behavior. A woman can grow in her ability to enjoy it as well as be creative in this physical area. She can learn to share her feminine charms with her husband.

Notice in the Song of Songs they both speak of her as a "garden" (4:16, 5:1). *"Let my lover come into his garden and taste its choice fruits"* (4:16b). She is not ashamed of her body and feminine delights; she senses what they mean to him. So she accepts her body, its form, its odors, its responses, as part of her God-given ability to satisfy him. *"How beautiful you are . . . with your delights,"* he says to her (7:6).

A wife will learn to be comfortable displaying her body. She will learn to dress or undress in a way that pleases him. She should not withdraw from displaying what she has to offer him.

When my wife, Ginger, speaks on this subject, she encourages middle-aged and older women not to hesitate to reveal their charms. "Not all of us can be a 10 (or have the perfect figure)," she says, "and age takes its physical toll. But, after all, your body is the one he has grown to love. Although it's familiar, it's a reminder to him of the countless past pleasures. The stretch marks and bulges are a reminder of the children the two of you have created out of your love. If you have become a little pudgy, remember how the master painters chose such types for their masterpieces." It is his body, too. *"I am my lover's and my lover is mine"* (Song of Songs 6:3).

Ginger also urges women to speak of their delights. Tell him you like what you do together sexually. Share with him verbally when something especially was meaningful or pleasurable to you. Men want to know their wives are enjoying what is happening between them. Ask our Lord to make you more and more the woman he needs.

Be patient. The inhibitions are not easily shed; the feminine sexual core is not easily released from its emotional shell. It may take years. It will develop, though, if you give it time, effort, and a willing attitude. The Holy Spirit, Who provides power to be in His image, will provide ability for you to be a woman in His image. Permit yourself to let go—to offer him not only your body, but the responses, the sounds, the spontaneous movements.

In much of these two chapters, I have dwelt on some of the more profound purposes of sex: its place in a couple's total oneness and its meaning for self-identity. You may be asking, Is it ever for fun? Does the Bible endorse sex for pleasure?

Invites Us to Enjoy

At first glance, it may seem that the Bible says a lot of negative things about sex. And it does. Because of the power of the sex drive, human nature is capable of perversive and damaging actions. Because of this there are many warnings about avoiding passionate lust and the *"sinful desires, which war against your soul"* (1 Peter 2:11). However, we must clearly distinguish between evil lusts and proper appetites. While fallen man and woman now possess drives that are sinful, they also possess appetites given to them at the creation . . . before sin.

Sinful lusts and desires are those which prompt us to use the sex drive wrongfully. Perverted lusts, acts of homosexuality, uncontrolled lust, adultery with a neighbor's wife—all of these are condemned. But none of these prohibitions are directed toward the pleasurable experiences God intended in marriage.

In the Proverbs of the Old Testament it states frankly: *"Rejoice in the wife of your youth. A loving doe, a graceful deer—may her breasts satisfy you always, may you ever be captivated by her love"* (5:18, 19). The word captivated is one used for being intoxicated. Here it refers to the emotional thrill of the sexual relationship in marriage. Acceptable pleasure and joy being associated with marital sex was a commonplace idea in Israel.

This positive stance toward sex is not changed in the New Testament. We have already cited passages which show that marriage is honorable and good. It is clear that sex is to be a delight to both women and men. While it is true that some may have a gift for remaining single, sexual abstinence is not forced upon Christians. In fact, though Paul commended the single life, he urges Christians to get married and express themselves sexually (1 Corinthians 7:1-7).

Our physical bodies testify to their capacity for sensual enjoyment. Our sexual appetites and apparatus were part of the original creation of man. A Christian medical doctor recently called my attention to how obvious it is that our bodies were constructed for sensual pleasure. A woman's clitoris, he noted, has no part in reproduction. Without it a woman could have intercourse, conceive, and give birth to a child. Yet it is one of the most prominent sexual organs in the female body. Its only function is related to pure sensual physical pleasure in sexual activities.

Both biblical and natural evidence convince us that couples should feel no shame in cultivating the sexual experience between them. And yet one author tells of how couples fail to do this.

> As the years go by, it is incredible to learn how many different items of apparel, positions, methods of achieving an orgasm, and the like become important to the sex act. Yet, strangely, the majority of older husbands and wives fail to exchange information about what excites them, and contrarily, what minimizes or destroys the sexual impulse.[2]

Sex can be made more enjoyable by making it more novel. Nowhere does the Bible condemn variety of posture and technique. What you do in the privacy of your own home is acceptable as long as you both agree and it is not harmful. Oral sex is acceptable by most Christians and pastors, according to a survey by author Tim LaHaye.

Variation in position and technique is not always necessary. Doing what satisfies both of you is what is most normal for you. There are other ways you can heighten the experience. Changing the circumstances will help. Making love in another place, such as a motel, will often make a great difference. Even another room of the house will sometimes make it special. In the Song of Songs, the out-of-door setting is closely associated with the couple's lovemaking.

By all means, it would seem best to enhance your sexual experience by building the total relationship. Sexual relating takes place in the context of personal relating. So it's good to include other expressions of intimacy with the physical: reading poetry together, listening to music, taking long hours to be in each other's sensual presence. Make your sensual encounters a lingering, wholistic experience of oneness.

Not that all sexual episodes will be the same. Sometimes they will be steamy and fiercely physical—at other times slow, lingering, and quiet. In his own unique way, the famous Christian author, C. S. Lewis, told of this variation in his own experience. After the death of his wife, during his period of grief, he wrote:

> For these few years H. and I feasted on love; every mode of it—solemn and merry, romantic and realistic, sometimes as dramatic as a thunderstorm, sometimes as comfortable and unemphatic as putting on your soft slippers. No cranny of heart or body remained unsatisfied. [3]

Delivers Us from Evil

Pleasure is not the only reason for the need to sustain the sensual part of marriage. The most explicit passage on marital sex in all of the Bible, 1 Corinthians 7:1-5, underscores another purpose of marital sex.

"It is good for a man not to touch a woman. But because of immoralities," the Apostle Paul says, *"let each man have his own wife, and let each woman have her own husband"* (7:1, 2, NASB). Once married, Paul counsels, *"Let the husband fulfill his duty to his wife, and likewise also the wife to her husband"* (v. 3). A husband and wife have a sexual obligation to each other. *"The wife does not have authority over her own body, but the husband does; and likewise also the husband does not have authority over his own body, but the wife does"* (v. 4).

What is most interesting about this passage is the reason Paul gives for maintaining a regular sex life. Marital sex prevents immorality. A good sex partner will help reduce the temptation to sin. Even couples who choose to abstain from sex, to devote themselves to prayer, should be careful not to stay apart too long. Paul warns that Satan might tempt them because of their lack of self-control (v. 5).

Thus you put yourself in moral peril if you deny yourself or your sexual expression in marriage. Sex in marriage is a duty. You are obligated to fulfill each other's needs in order to keep yourselves from being tempted. Paul says nothing about the repression of sex. He is more concerned that you express it so that you will not burn with passion (v. 9).

Expression or Abstinence: Which is More Spiritual?

This preventative function of sex in marriage should dominate a couple's attitude toward their sexual expression. This means that sex should be given freely. There should be no strings attached to the marital bed. Sex is not a favor to withhold, or a weapon to dominate. It is not a reward to be given for good behavior. Sex is something owed; it does not have to be earned.

It is unfair to force one's partner to repress his sex drive for pious or personal reasons. Paul does not say that a married person will be more spiritual if he is less sexual. We will show more love and spirituality if we are keenly interested in helping our spouse resist temptation by releasing his sexual energies.

Throughout the centuries, particularly in traditional Roman Catholic thought, abstaining from sex was considered morally preferable, even for married people. A marriage manual advised people that "perfect continence, perpetual over a long period, may be unreservedly recommended . . . on account of . . . its moral worth."[4] Too often this view led to mammoth dissatisfaction in marriage. Men with pent-up sexual desires sought mistresses. When sex went out of the marriage for the man, the man went out of the marriage for sex.

Paul offers no such notion to married couples. It is more spiritual to be concerned with your partner's sexual need. This is especially important when couples will have such a long married life together. With life expectancy as it is, most couples can expect to be together forty-five years or more. Unless they both dedicate themselves to continue and foster the romantic and sensual, it may become almost nonexistent as they grow older. This may force one of them to endure great temptation.

Helping Them Handle Their Passion

This passage of Scripture suggests that a married person should help his spouse handle his or her sexual passion. Sometimes one will be aroused when the other is not. This happens because couples are not usually perfectly balanced in their desires. One may seem to need more sexual occasions than the other. Or interest levels aren't equal whenever one is ill, under stress, or fatigued.

At such times, it may be better to help the partner release his passion than to feel it is wrong to do so. A wife can offer her body to her husband (which Paul says belongs to him). In turn, though, a man may not be able to perform sexually when not aroused. But he may bring his wife to a climax in ways other than intercourse if she needs a release. This will not be harmful if, in between such one-sided sexual episodes, there are those rich experiences where both are fully aroused and satisfied. When means other than intercourse are employed as expressions of kindness and consideration, these can contribute greatly to the closeness and love of married partners.

Duty, however, should not be the dominant feature of your sex life. Sex, like mountain climbing, can become a chore. It is only if we keep the meaning in the act that it will continue to be pleasurable and fulfilling. Permit the sexual abandonment of yourselves to each other to keep alive this force that continues to compel you to be one flesh.

Commune Occasion

Your openness in discussing your physical relationship together may be the most important factor to developing a fulfilling sex life. Therefore, the following agree-disagree exercise is designed to help you deal with the concepts of this chapter as well as share with each other what you think or feel. Try not to argue; rather, listen carefully to try to understand the other's point of view.

	Agree Strongly				Disagree Strongly
	1	2	3	4	5

Every couple should have and read a good manual on sex in marriage.

I respect sex because of its role in producing other human beings.

A man and woman can learn to become more interested in sex.

A woman's menstrual cycle affects her interest in sexual experiences.

A woman's orgasm always depends on her husband's ability to produce it.

A wife may not always have to have a climaxing orgasm every time she has intercourse with her husband.

One of the strong messages of sexual intercourse is that it says you are wanted and needed.

Sex is for oneness and oneness really makes sex worthwhile.

A couple should take whole evenings and even weekends to share together sensually and develop their sex life.

I feel somewhat guilty about having sex in marriage.

If a woman never has an orgasm, the couple should seek counseling.

	Agree Strongly				Disagree Strongly
	1	2	3	4	5

I especially like it when you say things to me that make me feel like a man or feel like a woman.

Romance is one of the things women most want in their sensual experience.

Physical variety and intensity is what most men want in their sexual experience.

Variation in positions is a good way to improve a sexual relationship.

It is acceptable for a man to desire and enjoy oral sex with his wife.

It is acceptable for a woman to desire and enjoy oral sex with her husband.

Sexual intercourse should be abstained from during the wife's menstrual period.

In order for Christians to cultivate their relationship in marriage, they should try to totally abandon themselves to each other in their sexual expression.

ENDNOTES

[1]Joseph C. Dillow, *Solomon on Sex* (Nashville, Tenn.: Thomas Nelson, Inc., 1977), pp. 94-95.

[2]Myro Waldo, *The Prime of Life and How to Make It Last* (New York: Macmillan Publishing Co., Inc., 1980), p. 40.

[3]C. S. Lewis, *A Grief Observed* (London: Faber and Faber, 1961), p. 10.

[4]Franz Von Streng, *Marriage* (New York: Benziger Brothers, 1939), p. 103.

CHAPTER NINE

WHEN PORCUPINES FALL IN LOVE
FACING CONFLICT

A friend of mine spoke with pride of the coffee stains on his dining room ceiling. "They are a symbol of the good relationship my wife and I have," he says, watching for my reaction. "In our marriage, we let out our anger. Sometimes we hurl cups at each other—filled with coffee."

His approach reminds me of a recent book titled, *The Intimate Enemy*. The author, George Bach, insists that "The family that fights together stays together." He explains how to fight fair in love and marriage.

Is fighting, however fairly, the Christian way to handle our marital clashes? Proverbs 20:3 advises: *"It is to a man's honor to avoid strife, but every fool is quick to quarrel."* And another proverb cautions: *"Starting a quarrel is like breaching a dam; so drop the matter before a dispute breaks out"* (Proverbs 17:14). On the one hand we are counseled to face our conflicts, but the Proverbs seem to suggest avoiding them. What is the answer?

Part of the solution comes when we distinguish conflict from quarreling. For most of us, quarreling is a negative word. It is associated with shouting and angry outbursts. A husband and wife square off like a manager and umpire on a baseball diamond. Quarreling is a substitute for more gracious ways of handling conflict.

Conflict is not the same as quarreling. *Conflict* is whenever two or more people have something come between them. It occurs whenever one person becomes an obstacle to the other. Quarreling is a reaction. Conflict is the basis of a quarrel. Conflict is inevitable; quarreling need not be.

When two people hurriedly weaving their way through a crowd at a shopping center suddenly bump, they are in conflict. The conflict will produce a reaction. Reactions will range from a kind apology: "Sorry," to an insulting question: "Why don't you watch where you are going?" or to physical abuse: giving the other an angry shove.

Biblical instruction deals primarily with the reaction to conflict. The Bible never denies the reality and legitimacy of human conflict.

Conflict is so basic to a relationship, it is impossible to have any closeness without it. The presence of conflict demonstrates you have a relationship. In Jesus' instructions on how Christians should deal with conflict, He said, "If your brother sins against you . . ." It is quite likely you will have trouble with the one closest to you.

Marriage is like two porcupines nestling up together on a cold night. You should expect, even welcome, conflict. You cannot get close without it.

Conflict Can Toughen a Relationship

I've stood beside a place where two mountain streams merge, excited by sight and sound of the bubbling, churning, foaming, and crashing of the swirling waters. When two individuals, like surging living streams, merge into one, we should expect the same results. Conflict is inevitable. Don't be surprised by it; be ready for it.

Anyone who has ever tried to live with someone else knows only too well how nearly impossible it is. One definitely married woman put it this way: "People discover they have firmly-held opinions on putting records back in jackets, and turning off the TV and not leaving soap to melt in damp soap dishes, and a million other things you never think about until you're living with someone who thinks differently than you do."[1]

The fact that we are sinful individuals is enough to cause plenty of ruckus in a relationship. Not all of these contentions are caused by our being sinful, though. They result from being different. We each developed our own unique habits, thoughts, and values.

Combine these factors with the reality that we must now live together, and we can make marriage into a combat zone. If we expect to get near enough to turn each other on, we ought to also expect to ring each other's bell as well.

The Danger of Avoiding Conflict

Having conflict is neither dangerous nor unusual. But avoiding it is. Couples who have split up after decades of marriage sometimes spent those years resisting conflict. When hearing of their separation, someone will often remark: "How odd! I never saw them fight. They were always so nice to each other." That was precisely the problem. They kept the marriage together by avoiding the issues. In doing so they also avoided each other. Peace at all costs—and it cost them their relationship.

This happens because too often the standard way of handling conflict is backing away from it. "Man would rather flee than fight," says psychiatrist Erick Fromm. Though there is plenty of fight in a lot of us, he has a point.

Faced with a discord, we tend to say "Aw, forget it." We say to ourselves: "Jesus said, 'Blessed are the peacemakers.' " We equate avoiding the issues with keeping harmony. One conflict management expert says he finds that Christians are very good at sweeping under the rug. Because they believe that Christians should love each other, they are ashamed whenever they end up as rivals.

It is possible that we are using Bible verses to cover up our fear. We are afraid of what we will say or do when we square off with someone. We don't want to hurt or be hurt. So we back down, back off, and eventually back out of the relationship altogether.

But resolving our differences is more Christian than running from them. We make peace by settling conflicts—not by pretending they aren't there.

Jesus said if your brother sins, you rebuke him, and he repents, *"You have won your brother."* Every time you wrestle through some divisive difference, you create a closer relationship.

Such annoyances are part of the repelling force in every marriage. Since all marriages have two opposing forces—attracting and repelling—you must learn to deal with both of them. You tighten your relationship by strengthening the attraction forces. All the while, you must deal with the repulsion side of the union: his eating habits, her constant yearning to go out, his meager sex drive, or whatever.

The Rock of Reality Instead of the Illusion of Peace

The marriage bonds grow tougher and stronger whenever you work through the conflicts that inevitably come. This doesn't mean you will successfully resolve the differences; it means you will at least try to talk them out and work them out.

Every conflict you avoid will not go away. It will still be around secretly, in each of your minds, like some evil spirit (Cupid's opposite) who wants to drive you apart. Unresolved conflict will show up in the still small voices that say: "Why did I marry that woman? How could I have fallen in love with someone so inconsiderate?"

These destructive voices will get louder and louder the longer you avoid really encountering each other about them. But once you do, you will begin to put them to rest. Your marriage will be stronger, because it will be built on the rock of reality instead of the sinking sands of deception.

One of my students invited me to breakfast to explain how this very thing had happened to him. I recalled the disastrous tone of his voice the night he called to tell me his wife announced she was leaving. For him, the end of the marriage was the end of the world then—death valley. What could he do?

Thankfully, they were both willing to duel. I sent them to a counselor who would be their referee. At last, after months of facing, not fleeing, he was telling me how new and refreshing their marriage had become. "I wish every married couple would go through what we did."

I understood. Their marriage was now not based on an illusion of peace. It now had the tranquility that follows the storm, not the deceiving peace before. He had found the trip through the cellar of conflict had turned out to be a journey through the tunnel of love.

Some Favorite Useless Reactions

Once you overcome the fear of conflict you will be ready to face it in a biblical, intelligent way. For one thing, you will avoid the negative ways of handling conflict. God's Word continually calls our attention to the many harmful ways we react to a conflict situation. *"Get rid of all bitterness, rage and anger, brawling and slander, along with every form of malice"* (Ephesians 4:31). *"Do not repay anyone evil for evil. . . . Do not take revenge, my friends"* (Romans 12:17, 19). *"A fool gives full vent to his anger, but a wise man keeps himself under control"* (Proverbs 29:11).

To sharpen your ability to see wrong ways of reacting to conflict, read through the following scenario. Does the wife handle it well? How about the husband's performance?

Skit: The Boob Tube Blues

[Wife is seated, reading a book. Husband enters briskly and says:]

Husband: *(shouting)* I'm home. It's wonderful me. Feeling great.
Wife: Hi, honey.
Husband: I used to dread Mondays. But Monday Night Football really puts a kick into my day. What's for supper?
Wife: *(Mutters to herself while slamming down her book and begins to walk out):* I'd like to put a kick into his day.
Husband: *(confused)* Wonder what's wrong with her? *(Picks up paper and sits down to read.)*

[Wife enters area where her daughter is.]

Daughter: What's wrong with you, Mom? You look like Jane Fonda at an anti-nuke rally.
Wife: *(she sighs, sits down)* Your father. He is so selfish. At times he makes me feel like a nuclear reactor that is about to blow.
Daughter: What this time?
Wife: He wants to watch Monday Night Football. I wanted to see the movie by that novelist I like so much. You know how I like historical movies.
Daughter: Why don't you tell Daddy how upset you feel?
Wife: It would only upset him, too. I can handle it. Though I must confess I wish he would think about me once in a while.
Husband: *(enters)* Hi, you two. How are you doing? Anyone want to bet an ice cream sundae on the game? I'll take the Dolphins.
Wife: *(mutters to herself)* You take the cake *(leaves for the kitchen).* Supper's ready.
Husband: What did you say? Cake? Are we having cake for dessert? That's terrific. I'll have a piece at half time, too.

Note, first of all, that their conflict was quite legitimate: it was over television and time. Many of our scuffles are caused by limited resources. Two of these are TV and time. We only have so much time to live and usually only one TV set. It's quite natural to disagree about hours and channels. Neither is he to blame for wanting to watch a sporting event or she a movie. The mission, should they wish to face it, is to work it out harmoniously.

Instead of doing that, they, like all of us, respond in ways that divide rather than unite. Do you recognize any of these in your closet of marital antics?

Withdrawal.   The wife in the skit failed to tell her desires to her husband. She communicated in roundabout ways that she was disturbed. She muttered to herself and banged her book to signal something was wrong. When he didn't get the message, she got hotter. But all the time she never directly dealt with the problem.

This withdrawal response is all too common. And there are many different reasons for it. I used to withdraw from interpersonal clashes because of my background. During my early years, my mother and dad fought regularly over a problem that was later resolved. Caught in the cross fire, I must have entered in my unconscious computer the statement, "There will be no quarreling in your marriage."

With this "no fighting" sign on the wall of my inner mind, I had a tough time facing issues in my own family. However, after experience and Scripture taught me differently, I took down the sign. You can't be a good parent if you aren't willing to face conflict. Kids will hand you plenty of it.

The woman in the skit was withdrawing, perhaps because she felt her husband would not understand. She didn't give him a chance, though. Or else she backed off because she thought a good wife should submit.

Submit she did, but with all of the reluctance of a rebellious kid. Like the boy who was told by his parents to sit down. He did, but grunted to himself, "I'm sitting down on the outside, but not on the inside." The wife was going along with him outwardly, but inwardly she was simmering.

She may have avoided being direct because she was avoiding being selfish. So she was indirect, hoping her nonverbal message would get through to him. Perhaps he would realize she might want to watch her program and then gallantly turn the knob to her channel.

Christians, in particular, may have this problem, this unwillingness to speak up for what they want in a situation. In the name of unselfishness, they keep their desires to themselves. Since it is more blessed to give than receive, they play the martyr, sacrificing all rights and demands.

But being a Christian does not mean surrendering all rights. Doing so may be the unkind thing to do. In this case the husband was not told of his wife's interest; he did not have the opportunity to give to her. There are times when we do give up rights and suffer being wronged (1 Corinthians 6 and 1 Peter 3:13ff), but that is more like a last resort than an initial response.

Too often our refusal to say what we want is not so noble. In this case, the wife did say she wanted something; but she said it unclearly, nonverbally. She felt sorry for herself, and thought: "He should have known I wanted to watch the movie. He ought to ask me first what I would like to do." Or else she feared her husband, afraid he would turn her down. If he did give in to her, then he would be upset with her for making him miss the football game. She was afraid he would sulk; so she sulked instead.

There may be a more subtle reason for not verbalizing our desires. Sometimes we believe that if we have to ask for something, it isn't worth having. We believe that if someone really loves us, they will know what we want and need. There is some truth to that. Isn't that the essence of the greatest of loves—mom's love. Isn't mother the one who always knows what we need even before we ask? She can discern whether the slightest of infant grunts means he needs to be fed at one end or cleaned at the other.

And so we grow up believing that if our mate really loves us truly, he or she will respond to our needs without our asking and demanding. Take, for instance, when I sensed my wife's tension in the early evening and suggested a back rub. "I appreciate you," she said as my fingers eased the tension from her shoulders, "because you always seem to sense what I need."

Too often we only sense what a person needs because that person is telling us so nonverbally. The intimate lover responds, then, to the nonverbal request. A wife, wanting to eat out in the evening, may not dare to ask. She communicates nonverbally: she sighs thirteen times, and explains she hasn't yet started supper.

Achieving the Impossible—Intimate Marriage

When a considerate husband gets the message and invites her to supper with Colonel Sanders, all is well. If he isn't too sensitive to the nonverbal or is too distracted to notice, then all is not well. The wife feels her request has been ignored even though she really hasn't clearly communicated it. And she may say to herself, "He should know how tired I am."

But should he? Aren't both partners responsible to communicate their desires to each other? And if one frankly says what he wants and the other gives, is that giving less significant than when the giving is done without the asking? Unfortunately, this attitude that makes us *go without* rather than *ask* produces more trouble than happiness in our marriage.

Involving a third party.   Because she did not have the courage or wisdom to directly face her husband, the woman in this skit vented her hostile feelings on another—her daughter. Whenever angry, bitter emotions clutter our insides, we get rid of them by talking about them to someone else. Another person becomes an emotional garbage dump.

The dumper will usually feel better. But the practice of saying to someone else what we should be saying to our partners will only do damage to a relationship. Not that we should always deny ourselves the confidence and assistance of a close friend. But talking to that person about our partner should never become a substitute for talking directly to our partner.

Reverting to sarcasm and slander.   The wife's mutterings, "I'd like to put a kick into his day," and "You take the cake" are sarcastic remarks intended to signal her hurt.

The Apostle Paul repeatedly warned against slander and filthy language (Ephesians 4:31) in spite of hostile feelings or attitudes. Slander, sarcasm, and other verbal attacks are a substitute for dealing with differences. It's a way of avoiding coming right out of the closet and saying what you really think and feel.

Blaming.   Probably more than any other reaction to conflict, blame is the most common. We accuse the other of getting in our way, of disrupting our life. The husband is denounced for liking football; the wife for not liking it. In reality, whenever no sin is involved, we are blaming the other person for being him or herself.

A person is attacked for being alive.

We condemn the person for being different. "If only you were this," or "If only you liked that," we think. We sometimes blame the person for not loving us because he or she is not changing fast enough. When a young wife is slow in developing her sexual responses, something she cannot immediately change, a husband may blame her for lack of love. This places almost impossible demands upon her.

It is unfair to insist a partner's love should enable that person to overhaul his or her temperament, habits, or personality at will. It's also a mistake to insist on this for the sake of compatibility. No two people are totally compatible. It requires time for each of you to become more satisfying to the other. In the meantime, the soreness caused by the areas of incompatibility must be regularly soaked in a solution of acceptance and tolerance.

Nagging.   Another very human response to conflict is nagging. The word nag, probably Scandinavian in origin, means to gnaw, bite, or hurt. It, too, subs for a sensible handling of bothersome matters.

The dictionary describes it as engaging in persistent petty faultfinding, scolding, or urging. It refers to causing distress by persistent small assaults. Several Old Testament proverbs refer to this practice: *"The contentions of a wife are a constant dripping"* (Proverbs 19:13, NASB); *"A constant dripping on a day of steady rain and a contentious woman are alike"* (Proverbs 27:15, NASB).

But men, too, are guilty of nagging. Instead of sensibly negotiating some course of action, we repeatedly harp on something. I do this about snapshots. The price of film and its development, from my viewpoint, makes photography one of the most extravagant things we do.

In one hour's time we can shoot with a camera enough for the price of a good dinner for two. Now I am not ignorant of Kodak's insistence that memories and snapshots are linked together. Richard Chalfen, an authority on photography, explains that taking pictures is a social glue, tying us together with people who may never be with us again because of death or moving or something else. I can understand this.

What I can't fully understand is what we do with the pictures after we have joyously carted them back from the drugstore. We each look at them a couple of times and then dump them into a drawer where they are forgotten. Well, not really forgotten—because I keep bringing them up to Ginger and the kids. "Why don't we do something with these pictures—put them in albums or something?"

Almost every time we pass photo albums in the store, I raise the same question. Whenever she or one of the kids want to buy more film for more pictures, I raise the question. I do it impulsively. And it's not really their problem. I don't even bother to put the snapshots I've taken into albums.

Someday, I hope, in our old age, we will have the time (or take the time?) to place them all neatly in albums and enjoy those endless evenings reminiscing. Sometimes I wonder if that will ever take place. So we go on snapping pictures and I go on snapping at my family. I don't like myself for it. Thankfully, they tolerate me. What I have been doing (nagging) is a poor substitute for getting us together and dealing with the matter.

Getting even.   Up to now, the responses to conflict we've discussed have not been too nasty. Yet we all are capable of violent reactions. Sometimes it is an undercutting, a getting even with our partner. We can get back at our partner by doing nasty things. Or we can get even by not doing what we should. Psychologists call this *passive rebellion.*

This showed up when I was counseling a couple married more than twenty years. He complained how she didn't care for the children or the house as he expected. She said he was a perfectionist. He continued his complaining, telling of incidents of neglect of the children, describing the continual mess that they called their home. While he talked, his anger level rose, his face flushed. Glancing at her for a moment, I noticed a slight smile forming on her face. She was enjoying his tirade. The less she did around the house, the more she got to him. It was her way of getting even for what he had done and been during their years of marriage.

What she was doing (or not doing) was cruel, but she felt justified. It is a fact that married people do cruel things to each other. Their bitterness and anger has replaced the affection they once had. They beat, hit, and kill one another. More people are killed in domestic quarrels than in any other type of murders.

I have come to believe that the ability to handle conflict in a marriage relationship may be the most crucial ability of all. In this chapter we have surveyed the how not to handle it; now let's look at how we can deal with it in the next chapter.

Commune Occasion

Discussion:

Because of your different backgrounds, you will probably have some differing feelings and ideas about conflict. It will be good to get these out into the open so that you can both understand each other as well as try to come to some mutual agreement in your views. Use the following discussion questions to prompt that discussion.

1. The chapter distinguishes conflict from arguments. Conflicts are defined as those times when we become obstacles to one another. Arguments are responses to conflict. Therefore, it is possible to have a lot of conflict in a relationship, but not resort to arguing to resolve it. Discuss whether or not you both agree with this distinction of conflicts and arguments.
2. Many people withdraw from conflict. Do you? Discuss with each other whether or not you are aggressive in facing conflict or whether or not you have a tendency to back away from it. Explain why you withdraw if you do.
3. This chapter suggests that it is all right to share with each other what you desire. For example, if a wife would like to eat out she should talk to her husband about it even if she fears he may react negatively. What do you think about this?
4. When you have a conflict, how do you feel? Try to explain to each other the kinds of feelings you have whenever you and your partner become obstacles to each other.
5. There are numerous useless reactions—besides withdrawal—to conflict discussed in this chapter. They are: talking to a third party instead of your partner, blaming, saying sarcastic things, nagging, getting even. Which of these do you have a tendency to do? Why do you think you do them?

ENDNOTES

[1]Judy Viorst, "Yes, Married," *Saturday Review,* September 23, 1972, p. 73. Used by permission.

CHAPTER TEN

HOW TO GET THE CASH OUT OF CLASH
HANDLING CONFLICT SUCCESSFULLY

"Talk to him about it," my wife Ginger counseled a young wife who was disturbed by her husband's behavior. "Let him know how serious it is." She gulped down Ginger's advice, got a babysitter, picked up her husband coming out of a building, and invited him to join her for dinner. He had been doing something that hurt her a great deal; yet he never realized just how much.

This distraught wife had been swallowing her bitterness, hoping he would somehow detect the problem and change. In the meantime she was watching and praying. There still appeared to be no change in his behavior or her emotional state. Now face to face she sat with him at a restaurant table. She announced: "We have a problem. Do you hear: We have a problem."

Was Ginger right in suggesting such a tactic? And was this wife wise in following it? Would the Apostle Peter have given such counsel? He urged wives to be submissive to their husbands. They were to adorn themselves with a *"gentle and quiet spirit"* (1 Peter 3:1, 4). To all Christians he said that *"if you should suffer for what is right, you are blessed"* (1 Peter 3:14).

Submission does not always demand silence, though. The example Peter refers to proves this. The Apostle chose Sarah as a model wife, saying she *"obeyed Abraham and called him her master"* (1 Peter 3:6). Sarah was not what you would call a silent wife, unable or unwilling to make her point when necessary.

In the Genesis record she came to Abraham on two occasions to claim her rights: once in regard to her maid, Hagar, and Abraham's son. The request on the second occasion, that he drive out the maid and her son, *"distressed Abraham greatly"* (Genesis 21:11). In her cultural situation, Hagar belonged to Sarah. Sarah had the right, then, to make these suggestions to Abraham. Making her request was not inconsistent with submission.

Confronting one another when you feel you have been wronged or when there is a conflict between you is both sensible and biblical. The strategies described in the last chapter are all substitutes for direct confrontation. We sulk, simmer, speak sarcastically, get even, and use all sorts of divisive and destructive devices—to avoid talking and working out our differences. And both husbands and wives do these things in the name of submission. We somehow feel that if we directly assert ourselves it is un-Christian.

Jesus was quite clear on this subject. *"If your brother sins against you, go and show him his fault"* (Matthew 18:15). In fact, Jesus prescribed direct face-to-face interaction if you were the one who did the sinning (Matthew 5:23, 24). Whether you are the sinner or the sinnee, you should handle the matter by direct confrontation.

Jesus follows the Old Testament principles in saying this. *"Rebuke your neighbor frankly . . . but love your neighbor as yourself"* (Leviticus 19:17, 18). Confrontation and reproof are not unloving. Refraining from making waves on the surface is not right when underneath there are flowing undercurrents of anger, bitterness, and disappointment. Such inaction is not a healthy way to handle strife and maintain long-range peace in your relationship.

Let's Face It

Confrontation is not a synonym for blowing your stack. There are some guidelines to follow for an effective confrontation.

Avoid a Crowd of Three

First of all, it should be a private affair. *"Show him his fault, just between the two of you,"* Jesus recommends (Matthew 18:15). Only if a person refuses to listen and the offense is a serious sin should you then bring others into it. This, of course, does not mean couples should wait until their marital troubles are gigantic before seeking counseling.

In the following passages, taking the problem to someone else is for the sake of discipline. *"If he will not listen, take one or two others along, so that 'every matter may be established by the testimony of two or three witnesses' "* (Matthew 18:16). We too often handle our individual conflicts in marriage by making them public. Our sarcasm and insults, even our show of ill feelings, crop up before our relatives and friends.

Joyce Landorf tells of the time this happened in her marriage. Early one morning she was helping her husband in the kitchen as they prepared a breakfast for the bank employees. One man, coming through the serving line, stopped to say he was impressed that his wife would so graciously climb out of bed before sunrise to help. Joyce's husband remarked: "Oh, that's just this morning; all I see most mornings when I leave is the back of her head." They chuckled.

Standing by, flipping pancakes, she overheard what he had said. She wondered why he would speak so sarcastically about an arrangement they had agreed to. Since he rose so early to go to work, they had decided that she would not get up in the early mornings with him.

While she thought about this, her husband got a laugh from another man at her expense. And he made the same remark to another. She knew she and her husband would have to talk.

Instead of sulkily criticizing or scolding him, she approached him with a more positive remark. "I didn't know my not getting up with you in the morning bothered you so much," she said. "Do you realize you joked about it with several men the other day?" This prepared the way for being honest.

He explained that though he had agreed to this, he felt something was missing because they did not see each other in the mornings. Whenever she was standing in the doorway seeing him off it did something for him; gave him a confidence and satisfaction. Underneath, he admitted he did resent leaving the house while she was lying in bed.

Their conversation not only cleared the air between them but led to a compromise solution. Despite the early hours, she agreed to see him off several days a week.[1]

Love It Up When You Bring It Up

Besides requiring privacy, confronting needs the warmth of love. For this reason someone has called it "carefronting." You rebuke, reprove, confront because you care, not because you are selfish or angry. Confrontation will help the other person as well as develop the relationship . . . even though it may hurt.

It's never easy to confront or be confronted. I was reminded of this just a few months ago. My wife, Ginger, was having a difficult time with me for a few days. I was depressed and discouraged over a matter and was quite out of touch with her. In fact, I was making her days miserable ones. She came to my study to discuss it. I rejected her coldly, even harshly—retorting I didn't care to talk. She left; and I could tell she was very upset. But I was too distressed to care.

A half hour later she came again. This time she didn't stay or try to talk. She simply said, "You tell us in your seminars that we are supposed to talk things out and tell how we feel. Well, you won't let me. So I wrote it down for you. Here!" She handed me a paper. I immediately saw her message consumed both sides. I stood there, paper in hand, wondering how I could refuse to face the issue. If anybody in this world ever had "asked for it," I had. Stunned, I read some of the most frank statements she had ever communicated to me.

What she said and why she said it were both underscored by love. It reminded me of the statement a woman once made: "Sometimes I write notes to my husband that say something like 'Frank, I hate you for what you did today. Love, Jane.' " The bottom line is love. Ginger had done it to help me and to help us; that I knew. I went to her. We talked, I confessed, she forgave, we prayed, and I grew and we grew—together.

Be Clock-wise

Along with love, timing is another important part of a good confrontation. Finding the right moment is an art. You can't expect the best results if you bring up a heavy matter when your partner is feeling down or fatigued. Strong emotions frequently drive us to say the right thing at the wrong time. Proverbs 25:11 mentions the need for proper timing: *"A word aptly spoken is like apples of gold in settings of silver."* Words pour out of our mouths to hurt rather than heal. It's as if a marriage is a license releasing us from common courtesies.

After a seminar, a woman gave me an example of sending ill-timed remarks. Her fire had been ignited at a women's meeting that afternoon. An elderly missionary, a widow, had spoken. At the close of the talk, she advised: "Be good to your husbands." Then in tears she added, "Mine died two months ago; oh, how I miss him and would love to have him around to do more for him. So go home; dress up for him; make him a special candlelight dinner; show him how you care."

The woman did just that—for the first time in two decades of marriage. He entered the door; she was full of anticipation, waiting to plant one on him. Without looking up, he plunked down his lunch pail and shouted angrily, "You drove the car over the grass at the edge of the driveway again." "He didn't get what I had planned," she told me.

Why are we so careless? Would that husband have handled the matter differently with someone who worked for him? Probably. Would he not have thought about when and how to confront an employee? Or a friend? Or his boss? Is a married partner due less consideration?

Give some thought to when you should bring up an issue between the two of you. Avoid times when your partner is down. Choose a moment when there is enough time to talk it out. Ease into it rather than making it so blunt or unexpected.

Give a Little Room

Confrontation may also be more considerate if the subject is presented as tentative. Unless there is a clear-cut sin involved and a sharper rebuke is in order, it would be better to share your perspective with less certainty.

David Johnson in his excellent book on interpersonal relationships suggests this. A husband could say, "It seems to me that you want to spend less time with me," rather than the accusing, "You don't want to be with me anymore." If we state it as a sort of hypothesis, it will give us both a chance to discuss the truth of the matter with less threat. It may give the person less of a need to defend himself or deny what you are saying.

Achieving the Impossible—Intimate Marriage

Resolve to Resolve

But confrontation is just the beginning of facing your conflicts. Together you must invent and adopt a satisfactory solution.

This step is the toughest. It is here where the hope for your marriage lies. It happens rather often that when a married pair discovers a difference, hopelessness sets in. It's like spooning out a fly from a bowl of soup; it's ruined the whole meal. What you thought was a near perfect relationship is not. But patience, understanding, and willingness to adjust will come to the rescue. You soon discover that a Christian must build a marriage on forgiveness and forbearance, not perfection.

"I'll Change"—Accommodation

Sometimes one of you will change for the other. The one who likes to go out a lot says, "For the sake of the relationship, I'll learn to stay home more."

I know many couples solve their conflict over bedtime this way. She is the "morning dove," liking to get up early in the morning and go to bed early. He is the "night owl," enjoying staying up late and, of course, sleeping as late as possible. Often one of the two is willing to change his habits over the years so that they can have each other's company in the morning and evening.

"I'll Accept the Fact You Won't Change"—Acceptance

Acceptance is sometimes the solution to the conflict. One agrees to accept the behavior and personality of the other. "You have been such a great husband, Jim," she says to herself, "I'll learn to walk through the piles of towels and clothes you create."

Sometimes the acceptance is about the same as toleration. You decide to "put up" with some aspect of your mate's life. I once had a woman challenge me on this point. She maintained that a Christian should not merely tolerate; from her perspective a Christian should accept. She went on to explain how she and her husband had come to accept having a severely mentally retarded child. At first, they painfully tolerated it. Now, after surrendering the matter to the Lord, it was different; they were happier, more at peace with themselves and God.

Though I understand what she is saying, I don't believe we must always come to the place where we have such an inner rest about everything. We can accept a person or a situation even if we are inwardly bothered. The Apostle Paul urged us to be patient, *"bearing with one another in love"* (Ephesians 4:2). That's the same Greek word used of Jesus when He said to His unbelieving followers, *"How long shall I put up with you"* (Mark 9:19). We can accept with consternation. Isn't this what Peter meant when he told us that *"Love covers over a multitude of sins"* (1 Peter 4:8)?

"We Will Both Change"—Compromise

There is another age-old answer to conflict: compromise. Conflicts need not always be resolved at the cost of one of you. Both of you can change. Both can be winners. In reality it is this middle ground on which the great marriages are built.

Though I am a night owl and my wife is a morning dove, we have not allowed this to separate us. Sometimes Ginger keeps me company late (usually by getting ready for it with an afternoon nap) and sleeps in with me. At other times I go to bed early with her. We are flexible. We have both changed through the years. Marriage is a compromise; we will compromise anything but our relationship.

A Built-in System

The solution of conflicts in your relationship should be as normal an event as your mother's crying at your wedding. You can build it into your lives. First of all, be sure you have a plan for resolving conflicts. Not all couples have such a strategy. They are taken off guard by matters they haven't decided how to handle. "After twenty years of marriage," a pastor said to me, "my wife and I now have worked out a scheme for doing so." One of the major features of the popular marriage encounter seminars is guiding the couples toward a process of conflict resolution.

Finding a strategy for conquering conflict involves establishing some ground rules. Choose the ones that you believe will work best for you. Though some may be unsuitable for your situation, you can use this list to stimulate your own creativity.

1. Stick to the subject; don't bring up other problems.
2. Avoid calling each other names. If there is a lot of emotion present, drop the subject and discuss it when you have cooled down.
3. Hold hands when talking about a conflict.

4. Have some signal for when the other person is insulting, unfair, or breaking one of the ground rules (such as holding up the right hand).

5. Don't use a third party in the wrong way, getting him to side with you.

Once you have a strategy, then have some agreement that will get you into the plan every time you have a conflict. The biggest hurdle is getting the discussion started; it's too easy to put it off, to sulk in our bitter feelings. Ginger and I followed Paul's advice in Ephesians 4:26 and agreed never to let the sun go down on our anger; by that we mean we would talk about the problem before going to sleep at night.

Charlie Shedd and his wife give each other seventy-two hours to be mad at each other. At the end of that time, the angry one is supposed to face the other. "Sometimes," he says, "one of us will come and say, 'I'm still mad at you; can I have a three-day extention?' But when that happens," he chuckles, "we sit down and settle it."

Developing the right atmosphere for talking about the dissonant notes of your marriage is also important. Ginger and I have some of our most frank talks around a motel swimming pool, where the aloneness and closeness give us the incentive and the time to talk things out.

There is absolutely nothing like praying together to create an atmosphere for dealing with issues. During our early married years, Ginger and I would get at a sort of impasse; we were discouraged, and it was hard to talk; we were confused and disappointed. Then I would say, "Let's pray." We bowed our sad heads and sometimes continued the discussion: "Lord, help Ginger to understand why I feel this way; help her to know that . . ."

When we lifted our heads, our sadness was replaced with hope. In a list of the factors that have given us the relationship we have today, praying together, praying together, and praying together would have to be the first three items on the list.

Do you have a plan for getting the cash out of clash?

How to Get the Cash Out of Clash

Commune Occasion

A Conflict Contract

Complete this agreement:

I, _____ , and I, _____ , have worked out the following plan for handling conflict within our marriage. We believe that it is best to face the problems between us and work on them instead of having them work on us. Therefore, we agree to the following guidelines:

1. Whenever one of us is angry or upset with the other because of some conflict between us, we will only permit _____

(number of hours)
before we mention it.

2. Whenever one of us is upset and the other one says, "What is wrong?" the one who is asked is obligated to _____
_____

3. Whenever a difference is brought up for discussion, we agree to hold to the following ground rules (select rules from page 129 & 130 and make up others that best fit the two of you):

   (1) _____
   (2) _____
   (3) _____
   (4) _____
   (5) _____
   (6) _____

4. Whenever either one of us does not follow one of the ground rules listed above (for example, starts to bring up other problems that are not relevant to the issue discussed), we will signal that person in the following way (select one):

   (1) Hold up right hand.
   (2) Turn around and face away from him/her.
   (3) Start whistling the tune to "The Battle Hymn of the Republic."
   (4) Other: _____

5. We agree that accommodation, acceptance, and compromise are all possible ways to resolve conflict and that we will never refuse to be open to discussing a problem with our partner.

6. If one of us breaks any part of this contract, he/she will be subject to the following:

   (1) Held to only one piece of pizza some evening (or one

potato chip).

(2) Be placed in the neighbor's doghouse (with the dog).

(3) Do the dishes for forty years (except on Christmas).

(4) Other: _____

Signed: _____   _____
          (husband)   (wife)

Witnessed by family pet this _____ day of _____ , 19_____

```
┌───────────────┐
│               │
│               │
│               │
└───────────────┘
```
(paw or claw print)

ENDNOTES

[1]Story adapted from Joyce Landorf, *Tough and Tender* (Old Tappan, N.J.: Fleming H. Revell Company, 1975), pp. 81-83. Used by permission.

CHAPTER ELEVEN

AVOIDING EMOTIONAL DIVORCE
WHAT TO DO WITH NEGATIVE EMOTIONS

Ginger once said to me: "I got an insight today into how I was feeling back then. Let me share it with you." Her statement doesn't seem too odd, does it?

The "back then" she referred to, however, was twenty-five years back. The feeling she mentioned was related to a problem we were then facing. It hit us during the first week of marriage and stayed with us for a number of years. The strong feelings it aroused in both of us made it hard to discuss and understand what was happening between us.

What is most remarkable about her statement is that she was still trying to identify just how she felt then. If she is taking twenty years to comprehend herself, it seems clear why I have trouble figuring her out.

The Trouble with Our Emotions Is When They're Troubled

Ginger has just as much trouble understanding me because we humans are rather complicated. Psychologists and psychiatrists train for years to decipher us. And even then, they sometimes sit back and scratch their heads.

We have the most trouble identifying and understanding our emotions. When the emotions are ones we label *negative*, they are especially hard to deal with.

Communicating emotions is easy when it is primarily positive. It's not hard for most of us to say, "Wow, you really look great!" or "I really feel so happy when you are around." It's built into us by our culture. Our love songs train us to share our good feelings. But when our lover makes us mad, it's not so easy to say, "You really upset me!"

These tough and touchy feelings are the major culprits that divide us. *"Get rid of all bitterness, rage and anger, . . . along with every form of malice,"* said Paul (Ephesians 4:31). He knew how divisive and powerful the dank, dark, emotional side of us is.

Not only do these feelings cause us to say and do things that hurt the relationship; but their very presence is a bother to us. When we have ill feelings we cannot share, we are denied a certain closeness. Not being able to say, "I am angry," means there is something I cannot disclose about myself. So I retreat into partially being a stranger.

This is precisely what happens to couples who once had such good communication but now are emotionally divorced. The warm, positive expressions flowed freely, right up to the wedding and beyond. Then there came the time when one irritated the other— more severely than was ever anticipated. The blow aroused hostility and anger.

Now the injured partner must care enough to say the very worst. The words stick in the throat. The subject goes untouched. There is a slight separation . . . a strangeness. Later another emotion will arise which they cannot discuss, then another, and again another. They will continue to retreat further and further from each other into their own inner world.

Dealings with Feelings: Recognition Instead of Repression

Denying Feelings Is Like Collecting Savings Stamps

First of all, Scripture clearly maintains we should be willing to recognize the feelings that we have. Paul says in Ephesians 4:26, *"In your anger do not sin."* Whatever a Christian does with his bad feelings, he should not ignore them. Be aware of the possibility of anger, Paul is saying, and do something about it.

Ignoring or denying emotions is such a natural response. We

say within ourselves, "A Christian shouldn't be angry, so I'm not angry." Or "A good wife should not be jealous; I'm not jealous." This may come as a surprise to some, but admitting our faults and true selves is distinctly Christian. Confession should be basic to the lifestyle of a believer. And it first means confessing to oneself.

Psychologists affirm what the Bible says on this. They warn against repressing feelings, denying they exist. When repression occurs, the feeling has a way of building up inside us.

One psychologist tells us it is like collecting savings stamps. Some people collect these stamps very carefully in order to redeem them for prizes. I have gone into redemption centers and seen people with neatly pasted up books of stamps. Each stamp has been carefully pasted inside each page. It is as if the person had little else to do than to sit and one by one fill up these books with thousands of these little patches of paper.

On the other hand, some people refuse to collect the stamps or do so carelessly. They toss them in the drawer or shove them in a pocket or purse with little regard. People do much the same with feelings. In certain areas or with certain temperaments they don't store up negative feelings. They slough them off and forget.

It is also human to repress them and continue to put stamps into our interior books. And then, one day, we get a full book and explode. It is as if we have been forced to believe we have a right to retaliate and redeem something for all of our internal suffering and anguish.

Treating Negative Feelings Like Labor Pains

Bad feelings are like labor pains. You can't stop what is about to happen by ignoring them. Unlike labor pains, though, hostile emotions don't result in blessed events. Their babies are little monsters. If you ignore the little fiend that is forming inside of you, look out! You may give birth to it without even expecting to.

This causes physical abuse in marriage. A husband allows the bitterness to build up, denying he could feel that way. Suddenly, when provoked, he strikes out. Paul warns against this: Don't let anger lead you to sin . . . deal with it.

Couples who suddenly separate may be the victims of repressed feelings. Like the woman who, at age eighty, went to a divorce lawyer to file for divorce. "After sixty years of marriage and eight decades of life, you want a divorce?" the surprised lawyer said.

"But why?" he asked. "Enough is enough," she unhesitatingly replied. The internal voice of many a person has whispered this, prompted by the neglected bad feelings of many years.

Sometimes the ill feeling will, like a volcanic pressure, push its way out in other areas. Feeling disappointed in the sexual relationship, a wife may complain of her husband's inability to manage money. Perhaps she denies her sexual frustration because she is ashamed of her sexual drive. Unconsciously, her anger drives her to attack him about their bank account instead of their marital bed.

Recognition, Not Repression

The human valve that releases the pressure is labeled: "Recognition." Simply confess it; admit it; recognize it. Say words to yourself like, "I really am bitter about his not getting home on time for supper." "I really am disappointed in our sex life." "I really am angry that she doesn't share her feelings with me."

One of the reasons we don't recognize our feelings is because we label many of them as bad or sinful. Even if they are, that shouldn't stop us. Our Lord encourages us to see the dark side as well as the right side of ourselves. We are too quick to label emotions like anger, jealousy, frustration as sinful. Paul clearly implies that it is possible to be angry without sin (Ephesians 4:26). We ought to be much more careful about this tendency to deny a feeling because of the thought that we have no right to feel it.

If we do deny that emotion, we also deny ourselves a chance to handle the problem. If a wife denies she is jealous, for example, she will not do anything about what is causing it.

I read of a wife who had this problem. After months of denying she was jealous (good wives don't get jealous, she kept saying to herself), she finally admitted the truth. Once she faced it, she began to analyze it. She discovered she was primarily jealous whenever her husband conversed with someone at social events. He talked with them about intelligent and meaningful things in a way that was absent from their relationship.

She learned that she was really not fearful of losing him or of his becoming sexually involved with another. Under careful analysis it all boiled down to this: She was jealous because she was being denied some good conversation with her husband. Recognizing the problem, she was then able to search for a solution. She decided to read the newspaper and periodicals to find intellectual matters she could discuss with her husband—and it worked. And once her need was met, her jealousy disappeared.

Human emotions, like pain, are indicators that something is wrong. Being aware of these feelings will make us more alert to problems in our relationship.

Reactions After Recognition

To Control or Be Controlled, That Is the Answer

Recognizing is only the initial step. Paul counsels, *"Do not let the sun go down while you are still angry"* (Ephesians 4:26). In other words, manage and deal with the anger. Christians are not counseled to let their feelings go, to allow them to control them. Some contemporary counselors may be giving unsound advice when they tell people to get the anger out. We need to be careful we don't surrender to our human passions in a way that the Bible warns us against. It is possible that when we vent our bad feelings by pounding pillows and shouting, we are involved in a process of generating more hostility.

Recognizing one's feelings should not include focusing such attention on them that the feelings are nurtured and thus grow to greater dimensions. *"Get rid of all bitterness, rage and anger . . . along with every form of malice,"* says Scripture (Ephesians 4:31); God cautions us not to nurse these babies into monsters.

"A patient man has great understanding, but a quick-tempered man displays folly," is a biblical Proverb (14:29). Another states: *"Better a patient man than a warrior, a man who controls his temper than one who takes a city"* (Proverbs 16:32). The Christian is to submit to the ruling of God's Holy Spirit rather than the hostile side of the human spirit.

A person can also deal with these feelings in practical ways. Physical exercise seems to be a good substitute for damaging ways of letting out pent-up emotion. If your marriage is causing you anger or frustration, a good exercise program will help you maintain some composure while you work on a solution.

Try Saying It with Words

Ill feelings also can be managed by verbalizing them. They are a lot like snowflakes which vanish when exposed to the warm light of day. Bringing them out into the open is best for you and your relationship. It's healthy to be able to say statements like: "I am upset with you;" "You have made me feel very disappointed."

We tend to avoid such verbalizing of feelings, choosing rather to express them nonverbally. We communicate how we feel by our actions, by the tone of our voice—by anything but words.

Why else do husbands and wives bang together pots and slam doors? Mostly they do it to signal their indignation. Sometimes couples develop clear-cut signals. If he slams the door between the kitchen and living room, he is upset; but if he slams the front door and walks out, he is really teed off.

Often counselors will describe couples who come into their offices by saying "they are not communicating." What they mean is that the pair is not talking. They are communicating . . . nonverbally.

They sit looking in opposite directions. Whenever they do glance at each other, invisible poisoned darts fly past the counselor caught in between. He knows it's his job to get them to say what is really happening inside each of them; then they can both understand the emotional depth of the situation. There are some solid reasons why couples need to learn to share those negative feelings.

Words Are Nicer.   First of all, saying how one feels may free you from the damaging nonverbal expressions. These can be quite serious. People reach out and slap, hit, and beat to show their anger as well as to get even. If you are able to say, "I am angry," it may make it less tempting to reach out and inflict harm.

Second, sharing will release you from the desire to make slanderous statements. Harsh feelings move us to hurt with sharp words. Instead of saying, "You annoy me when you do that," we tend to say, "You are so unthoughtful." We accuse the other person of wrongdoing instead of letting them know how they make us feel as a result of what they do. This doesn't give them a chance to explain . . . or to change.

Words Are Clearer.   What is most important about verbalizing feelings is that it avoids the ambiguity and distortion of nonverbal expressions. When someone speaks to you, face flushed, bent over tensely, a high pitch to the voice, and says, "Me, angry?

No, I'm not angry," you are getting a contradictory statement. Verbally, the person says one thing; nonverbally, another. It's confusing.

I go out with Ginger to a party. I believe we are having a good time. Out in the car afterwards, I turn the key to start the engine for our drive home. There is an icy feeling in the car; it is as if the snow is falling inside instead of outside.

I glance at my wife and say, "What's wrong?" And she says, breathing hard, stiffly looking straight ahead, "OOOOOH nothing." Nonverbally she is saying, I am upset; verbally she is denying it. It's like the dog that wags his tail and growls at the same time; you don't know which end to believe.

But I know that something is wrong. I don't know what or why. So I begin our multiple choice game. Was it because I talked too long with the blonde girl in the blue blouse? (Silence) Was it because I told all those old jokes again? (Silence) Now I am upset. If she is going to be silent, I'll give her the same treatment. We are deadlocked.

Sometime later I will get around to finding out what she was feeling and we will work it out. However, we are finding the faster we share what we are really feeling, the better it is for our relationship.

Words Are Accurate. Our nonverbal expressions are not that accurate. When we can't say how we feel it has a way of bringing havoc to the relationship. Take one of the most sensitive areas of all: sex. A wife refuses her husband's sexual advances as they lie in bed. Maybe she is feeling a bit separated from him and thinks his advances are out of place. Perhaps his male passion has shouted charge while her monthly feminine cycle has signaled retreat. But she may not have had the courage to say she doesn't feel close to him. So she says nothing.

Not knowing how she is feeling, the husband makes his most subtle approach. When she backs off, he rolls over and grunts. She is left lying there, trying to interpret what a grunt and 160-degree turn mean. Is he angry? That seems obvious to her. "Angry," she things to herself. "He has no right to be angry. All he thinks of is food, TV, and sex, not necessarily in that order." And now she is angry.

But suppose he is not angry. Primarily, he may be disappointed.

What a world of difference. Knowing he is disappointed should make her day! That's a great compliment to her. She should fear the day when he is not. If only he were able to verbalize it and say, "Honey, I understand, but I am disappointed. I'll get over it and there will be another time soon—maybe tomorrow night?"

Instead, they are left to their fuming at one another—permitting the sun to go down on their wrath . . . and the brightness to go out of their marriage.

How you speak your feelings may be as important as the fact that you do so.

It is important, though at times difficult, to verbalize them accurately. We don't always know how we feel; it's tough to distinguish between disappointment and frustration, anger and bitterness. Sometimes Ginger and I have to help each other here: I explain as best I can and she tries to help me understand what I am feeling, and vice versa.

Try Saying It When in Control

It's a good rule to wait till you are in control of your feelings before talking about them. It's too easy to say the wrong words when you are being driven by inner resentment. It would be best to say: "I am angry," when you are, than to say nothing at all. But it is better to back off and come talk after you have gained some composure. Talking about it the next day is healthy.

I often find the people who can't talk about their quarrels and disagreements when they are cool are the ones who have the most trouble relating. Some seem to only be able to talk in the heat of battle—like a blast furnace, they only operate when hot. You'll help each other understand a lot more if, after an encounter of bad feelings, you can later say, "Here is how I was feeling. Let me try to explain."

Verbalizing is also best when done without judgment, sarcasm, and slander. Sharing how you feel should be distinguished from attacking the partner. Say "Whenever you do that you make me feel very depressed," rather than "You never think of my feelings." If we judge we will fail to deal with the feeling and the problem causing it; we end up arguing about the judgment we have made.

If we can say, "I feel depressed," the conversation can deal with this. This is especially important whenever the feelings are out of proportion to the problem. Once a couple came to me about the husband's intense feelings of anger. As she sat beside him, he told how he was so outraged by some of the things his young bride did that he was afraid he would physically hurt her. It was over little things: not hanging up the towels, squeezing the toothpaste tube in the middle. His rage was completely out of proportion to what provoked it. And they both knew it. It was his severe response, not her actions, that needed to be dealt with. He would have to change. Together they would need to help him understand and deal with his temper.

The rule for handling bad feelings is a good rule for marriage in general: Be honest. The Apostle Paul says that Christians should speak the truth in love. Resorting to deception and dishonesty may sometimes seem like the easiest and best way to settle some issues. In the long run, deceit will turn your marriage into a masquerade dance where you eventually fear that taking off the mask will end the party.

We can too easily reach for lies like we do a room deodorizer to cover up the odors in the house. Eventually, dishonesty, like the deodorizer, will lose its effect unless the cause of the smell is removed. Nothing deals with those causes and clears the air like truthfulness.

Commune Occasion

How to Share a Negative Feeling

Example: Note that the following statements are really not all statements about feelings. Some are bad statements caused by bad feelings. But they don't really share what is being felt. The result is that the couple is unable to deal with the feeling and what is causing it.

Wife arrives late. Husband is angry and also a bit worried about her. When she arrives, what should he say? (Note, if he is really upset, it will be showing.)

1. Do you wear that watch only for decoration? Don't you ever look at it?
2. Why are you always late?
3. Sure I'm angry; wouldn't you be?
4. I get upset when you are late.

Number 4 is a clear statement of how a person is feeling. It is now possible to clear the air so that the man will not pout all evening and the wife will not keep guessing why he is acting so angry.

However, if the other statements are said, it will lead the accused to a defensive position and perhaps start a first class argument.

Number 1 is really not an expression of feeling. It is a sarcastic remark that is generated by the anger. It signals something is wrong, but it doesn't say it clearly; and it is not kind.

Number 3 is better than the first two since it does actually tell about the person's emotions. But it also judges the partner, putting her on the defensive. We often blame and judge people when we are upset. How much better to say, "You know I get upset whenever you are late; I know you'll try harder and I'll try to be more patient. Let's not let this ruin the evening."

Pick out the feeling statement in the following examples and discuss why it would be better for your relationship if you shared feelings in that way.

1. Husband not spending much time with his wife lately.

   (1) Why do you try to avoid me?
   (2) You're so in love with your job, why didn't you marry it?
   (3) I have been feeling quite lonely for you lately.
   (4) I'm fed up with your neglect of me.

2. Wife's seeming neglect of housekeeping makes husband very angry.

   (1) You know, they ought to give you a prize for being the world's greatest housekeeper.
   (2) This house is a mess.
   (3) I can't learn to live in a house like this.
   (4) I really get feelings of anger and disappointment when I see the house like this.

3. Wife doesn't pick up husband's cues that he wants to have a sexual encounter and he is feeling upset by her. She asks, "What's wrong?" What should he say?

   (1) Oh, nothing.
   (2) I was expecting you to be ready to make love tonight and I'm disappointed and a bit angry that you're not.
   (3) I can't understand how you can fail to see that I need you.
   (4) You wouldn't understand; forget it.

4. Husband makes his wife anxious because he spends a huge sum on a motor boat that she thinks they can't afford.

> (1) I'm O.K.; I'll let you manage the money and worry about the bills.
>
> (2) I feel anxious about our financial situation because of the expense of the boat.
>
> (3) I don't know why you throw money around like you do.
>
> (4) Great, buy a boat. Why not go out and buy your own lake to go with it.

If you were to follow the guidelines in this chapter, as suggested by Scripture and communication experts, you would choose to say the following from the above examples.

1. (3)
2. (4)
3. (2)
4. (2)

Of course, none of us is perfect; we will not always be able to say the right thing. The more we can do so, though, the easier it will be for someone to live with us and the better we will be able to handle those negative feelings that come between us.

Discuss how you would like your partner to express his feelings in situations like the above.

CHAPTER TWELVE

YOU, ME, AND HIM
DEVELOPING
SPIRITUAL
ONENESS

I once asked Ginger, "What is the way I show my love that means the most to you?" After being married to her for more than two decades, I was not expecting any surprises in her answer. She not only surprised me; she shocked me. She said, "When you pray with me and show concern for my spiritual life, that tops the list."

Ginger's answer shook me because it was so unexpected. What topped her mental list wasn't even on mine. I had considered my concern for her spiritual welfare as more of a duty than as an act of love. This new insight has changed my whole attitude whenever I pray and worship with her.

Our relationship to God should be woven into the fabric of our relationship with each other. Now each of us is composed of a personality made of many parts. We might be able to separate the social, physical, emotional, and intellectual parts of our personality in psychology textbooks, but we can't separate these areas in life. Our physical condition affects our social life. The emotional is influenced by the mental, etc. Whenever we act, or relate, we do so as whole persons. The interrelatedness of all these facets of our being is what makes the spiritual relationship so crucial.

The Apostle Peter emphasizes this tie between marital and spiritual life. He warns that if a husband does not live in a considerate way with his wife, giving her respect as a fellow Christian, their prayers may be hindered (1 Peter 3:7). It is not clear whether Peter is referring to the prayers of the couples or the husbands; but the connection between marital behavior and prayer is clearly there. How you relate in marriage will affect how you relate to God.

It clearly is the other way around: How you relate to God will shape how you relate to each other. Several prominent, veteran Christian counselors maintain that the practice of praying together is the most stabilizing factor in marriage. "Pray together—stay together" is not an empty slogan. One of them says that if he can get troubled couples to pray together, he has found the best remedy available for them.

The Sexual Connection

A couple's spiritual communion is even connected to their physical union. Nationally known marriage counselor, Charlie Shedd, maintains that prayer is one of the best turn ons for women there is. For years mankind has sought in vain for some pill or perfume to do this. Now many women are saying that the love potion is not chemical—but spiritual.

Shedd maintains that praying together prepares a woman for sexual relationships because sexuality and divinity are so closely related. There may be a more practical explanation. Praying together one on one is, after all, a very intimate thing to do. Numerous single young adults have told me that they have to be careful about praying privately with Christians of the opposite sex. It has a way of bringing them too close, too fast.

The sense of security that talking to God brings may be another reason why it makes for a good prelude to sex. Sexual surrender, especially for the woman, is safe and meaningful whenever the relationship is both safe and stable. Praying together assures you of your partner's commitment to God, before Whom you spoke your marriage vows. This assurance underscores his or her commitment to you.

The Tie That Binds

For these reasons, your spiritual practices together become a very powerful bond between you. Cultivating your spiritual union will be a critical part of developing your marriage.

All this does not infer that a good marriage is beyond the reach

of someone who is married to a person who does not share his
Christian experience. Dealing with this issue, the Apostle Paul urged
Christians who were married to non-Christians not to despair of
having a satisfying marriage. Though he clearly advised Christians
not to marry non-Christians, he just as clearly counsels those in
such a situation not to divorce the unbeliever. If the unsaved one
leaves, Paul advised, *"Let him do so"* (1 Corinthians 7:15). If the
unbeliever does not want to break the relationship, the believer
should not do so either (1 Corinthians 7:12, 13).

Paul was quite positive about the situation. He didn't see it as
half bad as much as he saw it as half good. *"For the unbelieving
husband has been sanctified through his wife, and the unbelieving
wife has been sanctified through her believing husband"*
(1 Corinthians 7:14). In such marriages, the Christian can have a
tremendous influence.

The Christian should not wallow in discouragement and self-pity
because he is denied the opportunity to share spiritually with his
partner. Instead he or she should try to live out the Christian relational
dynamics in such a way as to make it the best marriage possible.
The Christian's enriching contribution to the marriage will be the
best means of convincing the non-Christian spouse to become a
believer, says the Apostle Peter (1 Peter 3:1, 2).

Christians should take advantage of their unity of faith. Many
couples fail to maintain this divine connection. In a survey done of
our own seminary students, more than half the couples reported
they did not pray together even once a week. Along with what I
have learned from others, this survey confirms the fact that couples
have trouble tuning in to God unitedly.

For this reason, I would like to share some suggestions about
developing this area of married life which include some of the
problems couples have.

Make the Family Altar Portable

One of the major obstacles couples point to is time. Father
Time uses that big sickle to cut down all the good intentions to
have regular planned devotions as a couple. One of the ways to
solve this problem is to inject more spiritual experiences into your
everyday life. Our times of prayer, Bible study, discussions about
the Bible and spiritual matters need not be related to the scheduled

devotional time.

One of the unique things about the family altar is that it is portable. You can share God with each other any time, and any place. You can inject your awareness and communication with Him into any occasion. Whenever God commanded parents to pass on His Word to their children, He urged them to take advantage of the informal opportunities. *"Talk about them when you sit at home and when you walk along the road, when you lie down and when you get up"* (Deuteronomy 6:7).

Even though these are unplanned and spontaneous moments you can still work at making them happen. *Asking questions of each other* is one thing you can deliberately try to do. Raise thoughtful questions about issues that relate to your understanding of the Bible and life. Allow these questions to rise out of your reading, thinking, and reacting in everyday living.

You can deliberately do things to stimulate questions. Your attendance at church, special seminars, and lectures related to spiritual issues will promote discussion between you. Movies, TV programs you view, and books you read together will prompt you to talk about your morals, values, and attitudes. Plan to talk together over a cup of hot chocolate about how the book, movie, or TV program relates to your thinking about spiritual matters.

The intimate nature of married life provides a great context for spontaneous prayer and worship. Lying in bed in each other's arms after a lovemaking session is a momentous time to thank Him for bringing you together. Standing in the deep woods, by a lake or some other scenic place, you can join together in praising Him for His wondrous works.

Special occasions will also provide special times with God—an anniversary, your first day in a new home, the arrival of a baby. The impromptu worship in these contexts may be the most sincere of all. Like the Psalmist we can practice blessing *"the LORD at all times."* We can learn to say: *"His praise will always be on my lips"* (Psalm 34:1).

Plan a Time for the Three of You

Along with injecting the spiritual into the day-by-day activities, couples can also make a planned devotional time a part of their normal routine. This may be very difficult for some. I have talked with dedicated Christians who have no problem having their own personal devotions but falter when it comes to maintaining a regular devotional time with their partners.

One Relational Obstacle: Spiritual Maturity

Sometimes the problems are relational. A frequent hindrance is the spiritual maturity level of each. Often, one partner is ahead of the other. This is particularly troublesome when the woman is the one who is more advanced.

Though he knew he married an angel, he is threatened to find she is an archangel. She can quote whole Psalms while he still struggles to remember just how John 3:16 begins. And when they discuss theology, she mentions Calvin, Warfield, and Arminius as if they were members of the Dodger bullpen. Part of the problem is that it is downright embarrassing. When reading Scripture, he stumbles over words like Amalekites, Ammishaddai, Uphaz, and Areopagus. She obligingly helps him with the pronunciation as if they were household words to her.

Whether it is the wife or the husband who is out in front spiritually, numerous couples seem to see this as a problem in their relationship. It should not be. This spiritual imbalance should not be permitted to hinder your spiritual sharing. If it does, you need to talk it out. Perhaps the more "mature" one is giving out signals of superiority. Though they are not deliberate, they still make the other one feel unaccepted, inferior, or even guilty. The bad feelings cause this partner to back away from the intimidating "devotions." Or the "less mature" one may be at fault. He or she may have too competitive an attitude, lacking the humility that is necessary to learn from the partner.

Partners who discover they are not on the same level of spiritual maturity should be very careful not to allow this to damage their spiritual relationship. In many of these cases the less mature Christian drops out of the spiritual involvement and the gap in their spiritual level becomes even wider. Wise Christians will work hard at overcoming any barriers to growing together and cultivating the experience of being *"heirs with you of the gracious gift of life"* (1 Peter 3:7).

Another Relational Obstacle: Intimacy

Another relational barrier to having couple devotions has to do with intimacy. Because praying together is such an intimate experience, some persons are very uncomfortable doing so. While praying out loud together may be as easy as talking about the weather forecast for some couples, it is very difficult for others.

Dedicated Christian men have told me that they didn't pray much with their wives because it was so hard to do. Whenever they prayed, they got very open and honest with God; their relationship with their wives had not developed to the place where they could do that comfortably in their presence. The green relationship of man and wife needs time to ripen before such spiritual interrelating is possible. It sometimes takes years.

Like other obstacles, you can overcome them and develop a fulfilling spiritual oneness.

Suggestions for Spiritual Sessions

The following suggestions are made with the realization that the development of spiritual oneness is not easy. As Christians, we know there will be three major forces resisting us: the world, the flesh, and the devil.

The world opposes us with numerous attractions that compete for our time and distract us from God's value system. The flesh will resist us by its silly preference for the glittering, empty things, by its laziness, its pessimism. And somehow Satan will work to keep us from God. James suggests we will need to resist the devil if we are going to draw near to God (James 4:7, 8). Perhaps the following guidelines will help you do that.

Pencil It In

If you have ever read any guide to having devotions, or heard a talk about it, you have encountered this suggestion before: Schedule them. In the same way a baseball player won't get to the plate without being in the batting order, you won't get to first base in spiritual oneness without placing it on the calendar. Remember this: A schedule is not designed to make us heap mountains of guilt upon ourselves if we don't perfectly keep it. A schedule is not a shackle to enslave us.

Schedules are made to be broken. We remain flexible, permitting the unpredicted to veer us from the course we had set earlier. We do know that we will get more accomplished if we plan ahead. A schedule is a sort of robot tour guide that we program in our saner, more thoughtful moments. It pays to listen to him. When the Psalmist said *"teach us to number our days,"* he wasn't exactly telling us to make a slate of the day's activities (Psalm 90:12). He was suggesting that we ought to give thought to how we use our time.

Nor should a scheduled time keep us from enjoying the more spontaneous times I've mentioned earlier. Place in your schedule the time when it is easiest for you to have devotions as a couple. Choose a time when your attitude and energy level will make it work.

Easy Does It

Make your devotions simple and brief. Simplicity will make it more possible and brevity will make it more realistic. I have heard engaged couples discuss plans for their devotional times which will begin after the wedding. They planned to give at least an hour a day to joint study of the Scriptures and prayer. Sadly, I have also heard them tell of how soon their elaborate plans became obsolete.

It's too difficult for people to study together for such a long period of time. Our educational experiences don't prepare us for it. We are accustomed to studying alone or in a discussion group, but not in a one-to-one dialogue.

Life's demands and constant interruptions also make it hard to keep up such ambitious plans. The big plans turn into no **plans** at all. Planning to do too much will eventually lead to doing too little.

For couples just beginning devotional times, I would recommend reading a short passage of Scripture, discussing it, and then praying together. Permit the discussion time to lead you in any direction. You may end up spending a whole hour in a lively discussion. Sometimes the talk will be painfully difficult and slow. You may want to use a devotional guide of some sort. A recently released book, *Together Each Day,* by Joan and Bill Brown, is brief and simple enough for any couple to use. It would make an excellent beginning book.

Horizontal Is Good, Too

Being in touch with God does not exclude being in touch with each other. It's beneficial if you make your time of relating to God include your relating to each other as well. Christ nourishes us through one another. As you are open to each other, you will be opening yourself up to Christ within one another.

In-depth sharing and listening can become an essential part of your devotional time. You can initiate such sharing in the discussion of the biblical passage. You can get personally involved with each other by the kinds of questions you pose.

Suppose you have just read Psalm 31 which contains these words:

> *Be my rock of refuge,*
> *A strong fortress to save me.*
> *Since you are my rock and my fortress,*
> *For the sake of your name lead and guide me . . .*
>
> *Be merciful to me, O LORD, for I am in distress;*
> *My eyes grow weak with sorrow,*
> *My soul and my body with grief.*

You can always raise the intellectually oriented questions: "What is a strong fortress?" "What does he mean by comparing God to a rock?" "What does the word 'distress' mean?"

Then more personal questions will enrich the time. "Do you think it is all right for a Christian to grieve?" "What makes you feel distressed?" "How can we help each other at times like these?"

You can especially become more intimate if you deal with questions about feelings. "What do you feel about this passage?" "Do you ever feel like the Psalmist?"

This personal touch will brighten up your devotions as a couple. You will be more motivated to get together at these times if you know that you will not only be meeting God, but each other.

Tied to Reality

Relating your devotions to the rest of life will also enrich them. Our spiritual times can be too isolated. Sitting down to read the Bible and pray is like an interruption to the flow of life. This is true because the biblical materials of yesterday sometimes seem too unrelated to what we are doing today. It's tough to switch from watching TV or sanding a chair to getting excited about Elijah's squabbles with Jezebel, even though you know it comes from the Word of God.

To overcome this we will need to work at making our

devotionals fit into what we are presently doing and thinking about. One of the ways we can do this is by taking some biblical truth we have already been thinking about and making it the basis for our discussion.

As I mentioned earlier, we could use Monday's session to discuss the passage of Scripture from Sunday's sermon. Instead of trying to warm up together to another section of Scripture, we can interact about one that is already fresh in our minds. Or we may start our devotions by thinking about a current issue and then going to Scripture for an answer. Or else we can talk about how that problem related to what we know about our faith.

In other words, the devotional times need not always begin or be centered about a passage from a book or from the Bible. It can center about what we are currently confronting. Our devotions as a couple are an attempt to help each other grapple with life. The closer these sessions are to contemporary reality, the easier it will be to get into them and make them meaningful.

Celebrate

Inject a celebrational element into your spiritual relationship. Perhaps one of the reasons we back away from devotional sessions is that they get too heavy. We tend to focus on the problems. This might be because our church prayer times often follow this pattern. We begin with the requests which usually center around the tragic: a crippling auto accident that someone heard about at work, a gory operation someone's friend's second cousin had. Then, we get reports of revolutionary coups and missionary setbacks in distant nations whose names we can hardly pronounce correctly. By the time the list is formed, we are not too convinced God is still in business on planet earth. It can be downright depressing.

As couples, we can let the same thing happen to us. We drag out all of the problems we can think of and end up feeling negative about life. Not that we shouldn't pray about such tragic difficulties and remember the people caught up in them. But we should also reflect on the good things that are happening. When the Apostle Paul ugred us to pray about everything, he added the phrase, *"with thanksgiving"* (Philippians 4:6).

Instead of merely dredging up all of the awful and negative things in life, we can intentionally be more cheerful. Celebrating God's gifts and His works puts us into a positive frame of mind and encourages our faith. We can do this by asking questions: "What happened today to make you glad?" "What did someone say today that made you feel great?" "Where during the last few days did you see God at work?"

Perhaps your answer will not qualify for a Guinness Book of World Records, but if it was good to you, it will be worth sharing with your partner. Ginger and I have used sentence prayers to develop this positive attitude. "Lord, I feel good about . . ." or "God, what I appreciate about today is . . ." "Lord, what I saw or experienced today that makes me happy to be alive was . . ." "Father, what I appreciate in my relationship to my partner is . . ."

Learn to celebrate. It will add a joyful flavor to devotionals . . . and all of life.

A Touch of Cinnamon

Putting some variety into your devotional times will also season them. Just a bit of planning and creativity will make this possible. It's not hard to do on a periodic basis. Decide ahead of time to spend four or six weeks reading a certain devotional guide. See those suggested in the reading list at the end of the book. You can then plan to switch to reading through a book of the Bible for the next month or so. Later you could read out loud an uplifting book.

Variety can also be injected into a weekly schedule, if you decide to have daily devotions. Mondays could be given to discussing the Bible passage used in Sunday's sermon. Tuesday: reading a devotional book. Wednesday: having a praise and prayer session. Thursday: reading missionary letters and praying about their contents. Friday: reading from the devotional book, etc.

Personalize

The most important ingredient to successful spiritual interaction is your making the time personal. You should permit your uniqueness to dictate what you do. While you may want to consult some devotional guides and consider suggestions like you have just read, you will need to do what is most comfortable and best for you.

Some couples are too embarrassed and too threatened to pray out loud together. You can prevent this from robbing you of spiritual communion by praying in other ways. Perhaps you could discuss a prayer request and then pray silently in each other's presence. Or you may feel free to read prayers out loud. Some devotional guides include a written prayer. The Psalms in the Bible and songs in hymnals are also very suitable for reading in prayer together. These beginning practices may eventually make you comfortable in praying your own words while in each other's presence.

Marriage Yeast

Whenever anyone asks me what is the one most important facet of a Christian marriage, I answer quickly: spiritual oneness. If building a marriage were compared to baking a loaf of bread, the one ingredient that would compare to yeast would be the spiritual togetherness. More than anything, how you relate to God may determine whether or not your marriage rises successfully or falls disappointingly flat.

Commune Occasion

Developing Our Spiritual Togetherness

Handling the Hindrances

Which of the following is the most significant hindrance to your having prayer, Bible study, and other forms of spiritual togetherness? (each of you write this on a piece of paper, then compare and discuss your lists):

Time
Willingness to be open
One of us is embarrassed
One of us feels spiritually inferior
Lack of planning
Not seeing the value
Not making it a priority
Just haven't worked hard enough at doing so
Conflict over method
Too boring
Distractions (children, phone, limited time alone)
Fear of failure
Don't know what to do
Lack of discipline

Different ideas about Christian faith

Other _____

Probing the Potential

Which of the following ideas of this chapter appealed to you?
(Write down your answer, and then compare and discuss.)

Praying silently together

Reading prayers, like the Psalms

Praying spontaneously, as on a walk in the woods or after
making love

Discussing Sunday's sermon

Talking about feeling prompted by what we read in the
Bible

Discussing the biblical passage together

Reading together through a whole book of the Bible, a bit
each day

Reading through a devotional book

Using sentence completion sentences to do some
celebrating of what God has done for us . . . such as
"Lord, I feel good about . . ."

Making the devotional aims simple

Having variety by planning to do different kinds of
devotionals for a month or so (like reading a book of
the Bible) and then going to something else (like
reading a devotional book), etc.

Having variety during the week; planning something
different for each day

Planning the Probabilities

Using the above discussion as a guide, do some planning of
what you would like to try doing for the next month of devotional
times together.

CHAPTER THIRTEEN

CAN WE ROLE INTO A HAPPY MARRIAGE?
UNDERSTANDING HEADSHIP AND SUBMISSION

W hen Lady Diana Spencer married Prince Charles, he became her lord, but not her master. The couple broke with the precedent of royal weddings. For the first time, the royal bride did not make the traditional vow. She promised to "love him, comfort him, honor and keep him" but did not agree to obey him.[1] Now even a Prince's home is not his castle.

If modern ideas of marriage have reached the traditional British royal family, they have gone a long way. It is another clear signal that past ways are giving way to new ones.

In a recent magazine article on how women's roles are changing, *confusion* was the major word. Because women were changing their roles, men were uncertain about theirs.

But this modern state of things is not exactly fresh on the scene. Even when societies gave clear signals about how husbands and wives should play the game of marriage, couples had power struggles. Literature old and new is loaded with accounts of husband-wife squabbles as well as jokes about them. "My wife and I have a good arrangement. I make the big decisions and she makes the small ones. It works well; we've been married for twenty years and have had no arguments. Actually, we haven't had any big decisions either."

Apparently people throughout history have laughed about this marital power and the ploys devised to relieve the pressure that builds up inside marriages. The struggle for power is so out of place between two people who are in love with each other. Marriage resists being forced into a sort of business arrangement between a ruler and his subject, since it is really a relationship between lovers.

It is precisely because of this that some question whether the Bible designates clear-cut husband-wife roles, and what these roles should be. Some evangelicals challenge the traditional submissive role for the wife. They shift the emphasis to mutual subjection: in Christian love husbands and wives are to submit to each other's needs. Pat Gundry states: "A marriage based on the principle of mutual submission goes beyond roles and formulas and makes them unnecessary. It becomes a marriage of equal persons and makes the intimacy so many people are longing for today."[2]

Does the Bible prescribe specific roles for a husband and wife? Did God design that the wife should submit to her husband? And if so, will these roles interfere with their close relationship? Christian couples will want to examine the various viewpoints in an attempt to arrive at their own answer. While it is good for each of them to agree with the other on the matter of roles, it is better for them to be convinced that their position follows the guidelines of God's Words.

Equal Persons—Equal Power

Those who challenge the traditional roles call themselves *egalitarians.* They hold that marriage is a democratic arrangement. Husband and wife, being equal before God, are equal before each other. Power is split fifty-fifty. Each partner is as free to pursue a career as the other.

They offer a biblical basis for this position. They maintain that man and woman were created as equals. It was only after the fall of man into sin that man was declared to rule over the woman as a judgment. Jesus Christ has now canceled all of this through His death on the cross. *"There is neither Jew nor Greek, slave nor free, male nor female, for you are all one in Christ Jesus,"* writes Paul (Galatians 3:28). Since a husband and wife are equal in Christ, there is no foundation for differences in roles in marriage.

Can We Role into a Happy Marriage?

Doing Away with the Traditional Script

This leaves egalitarians to grapple with a number of New Testament passages which seem to suggest that the husband is to be the head of the home. Paul commanded this subjection in his letter to the Ephesians: *"Wives, submit to your husbands as to the Lord. For the husband is the head of the wife as Christ is the head of the church. . . . Now as the church submits to Christ, so also wives should submit to their husbands in everything"* (5:22-24). Peter also urged submission in one of his letters: *"Wives, in the same way be submissive to your husbands. . . . Like Sarah, who obeyed Abraham and called him her master"* (1 Peter 3:1, 6). The egalitarians primarily maintain these passages are adapted to the social practices of biblical times. Women were to go along with culture just as slaves were to submit to the current system of slavery, even though the Gospel declared there was liberty for both of them. Submission in these cases was an act of Christian love.

But egalitarians have trouble treating all the husband-wife passages in this way. Sometimes Paul gives reasons for submitting that are not bound up in culture. He says that the husband is the head of the wife as Christ is the head of the church. When Paul compares Christ's headship to the husband's headship, he seems to be giving some substantial reasons for a special role of the husband in the home. Nowhere does Paul give any such reasons for slaves to submit to their masters. In other words, Paul does not give theological reasons for slavery; he seems to do so for the headship of the husband.

Doing Away with Theology

In response to this, defenders of the fifty-fifty position try to do away with the theological reasons in these passages. The statement of Ephesians 5, *"The husband is the head of the wife as Christ is the head of the church"* is dismissed by redefining headship. Headship, they say, does not mean leadership. Headship in New Testament times refers to something else: The head is a source of nourishment. In the passages that speak of Christ's headship, Pat Gundry concludes, "Christ is a loving, serving, uniting, nourishing, sharing Saviour."[3] When headship is applied to marriage it means the husband is to be provider and protector, not leader.

Dismissing the argument of chapter 5 of Ephesians does not

dismiss all of the theological arguments for the husband's leadership. In 1 Corinthians 11 the Apostle Paul bases the different roles of husband and wife on two arguments: *"for man did not come from woman, but woman from man,"* and *"neither was man created for woman, but woman for man"* (1 Corinthians 11: 8, 9). In doing this, the Apostle Paul sees the differences between husband and wife coming out of the creation passage, Genesis 2. Therefore, since egalitarians deny that the different roles are based upon creation, this passage is quite damaging to their position.

Attempts to handle this passage vary in approach. Paul Jewett gives the most forceful argument, but in the process, he shows less respect for the inspired Scriptures than do evangelicals in general. He says that these arguments of Paul were part of his thinking as a Jewish rabbi. In this passage, he is struggling over which is right: his new revolutionary position in the Christian faith or these rabbinical ideas. Jewett in this way maintains that we as Christians cannot follow these arguments.

Equal Persons—Different Roles

Disagreeing with these egalitarians, many evangelicals take a more moderate view of roles in marriage.

They believe the husband has a leadership role in the home, but they try to discover some middle ground between the egalitarian position and the extreme authoritarian position, which was rooted in the seventeenth and eighteenth century European culture. At that time, the wife was more or less the property of her husband. She may have been called the "better half," but he got the better deal.

This excessive, almost dictatorial view is still around. One fundamentalist minister counsels the women of his church to allow their husbands to beat them in checkers to help bolster the male ego. And one speaker gives this advice to wives: "How do you overcome the fear of your husband driving too fast? Recognize that God is in control and whatever happens is within His will. . . . Remember also the "Father-filtered" principle and as Mary might suggest, 'Pray for a policeman.' "[4]

A biblical position of submission does not condemn the wife to endless losses of checker games or helpless silence beside some maniac at the steering wheel. Those of us in the middle position believe these suggestions take the concept of submission further than it should be taken. Submitting is not equivalent to servitude because headship is not equal to dictatorship.

Explaining the Biblical Basis

The solid, biblical foundation for a husband's leadership makes us unwilling to give it up for the egalitarian viewpoint. It arises, first of all, out of the fact that God so clearly says the husband is the head of the wife. Egalitarian attempts to bleach out of the term "headship" any idea of leadership seem futile. Granted, headship does refer to being a source of nourishment and strength. But egalitarians overlook other statements related to it. Speaking of Christ, Paul associates authority with headship: *"And God placed all things under his feet and appointed him to be head over everything for the church, which is his body"* (Ephesians 1:22, 23). And when comparing Christ headship to the husbands, Paul makes it quite clear he is talking about leadership. *"Now as the church submits to Christ, so also wives should submit to their husbands in everything."*

Those of us who hold to this headship-subjection arrangement also point to the reasons the New Testament gives for it. In a passage already pointed out, 1 Corinthians 11, we see that Paul bases his ideas on the creation account: *"The head of the woman is man. . . . For man did not come from woman, but woman from man; neither was man created for woman, but woman for man"* (1 Corinthians 11:3, 8, 9). If Paul were merely counseling Christians to go along with their cultural customs, he would not have given reasons based on the Old Testament.

Egalitarians argue that the assignment of different roles makes men and women unequal. Those in the middle position claim this isn't so. They maintain God created husbands and wives as equal; but also different. There is nothing illogical about making one person a leader among equals. Paul did not have any trouble stating that *"the head of Christ is God"* (1 Corinthians 11:3). Yet, we consider the Father, Son, and Holy Spirit as equals. Nor does our being under church leaders make them superior to us (Hebrews 13:17). Different roles in a marriage relationship do not deny that husband and wife are joint heirs in Christ. Christian husbands and wives are different individuals who complement, not compete with each other.

Looking at an Unkind Past

Headship, then, is based upon how God created us. It is not a result of man's sinfulness. Unkind, autocratic, oppressive treatment of women comes from mankind's sinfulness. When God predicted the husband would rule over the woman because of the first sin, He was describing what would happen because of the fall of humanity.

Sinful males tend to dominate women. Even past Christians harbored dismal attitudes toward women. Tertullian, in the third century, said to the women of his congregation:

> And do you not know that each of you is an Eve. The sentence of God is on your lives in this age; the guile must of necessity be too. You are the Devil's gateway; you are the unsealer of that tree; you are the first deserter of the divine law; you are she who persuaded him whom the devil was not valiant enough to attack; you destroyed so easily God's image, man. On account of your dessert— that is, death—even the Son of God had to die.[5]

It is possible to dredge through the slums of church history and bring to the surface scores of bitter statements attacking woman as evil, a disciple of the devil, a fountain of deception and even "rust corrupting the saints."[6] Certainly the New Testament deplores this view of women. Yet it assigns leadership responsibility to the husband, not as a judgment, but as something that arises out of God's will in creation.

Once we put the marriage roles in a proper biblical light, we will rid them of the damaging excesses of some evangelicals as well as answer the complaints of egalitarians. Standing in between these positions, many of us see the following characteristics of those roles.

Headship—Not a Head Trip

Headship is not an honor or privilege; it is a responsibility. God assigns man the role of leader for the function of the family. He should initiate activities and discussions and guide the affairs of the family. Yes, he will have the last word, but he also has the duties that go with it. His role is not an opportunity to get what he selfishly wants. His wife is a helper, not a slave. The Hebrew word for helper is used of God more than of anyone else in the Old Testament, proving its use does not suggest inferiority.

Our homes need leadership. A power vacuum, not a power struggle, exists in most of them. The modern husband may be more apt to abdicate than abuse his position. Women are forced into taking responsibility they often don't want. Psychologist Lawrence Crabb says that husbands are inclined toward the "don't bother me" attitude. Coming home from work, they fall into a reclining chair rather than into a throne.

A moderate view of headship claims the family is a small group that needs leadership. The man is appointed to give it. If he doesn't take the role, the wife will have to do so. Some experts maintain that the idea of shared leadership is not much of a reality even among those who want to have it. In their study of how roles resolve conflict, Dr. David Olson of the University of Minnesota and Robert Ryder of the University of Connecticut discovered that although eighty percent of the couples interviewed said that they shared leadership in their marriages, only twenty percent actually did.[7] Harmonious music from a marriage or an orchestra partly results from someone leading. The Bible suggests that a loving husband is assigned to this role. Isn't this better than having two people striving, consciously or unconsciously, for power, ending up being dominated by one or the other?

The Head Ship Is the Love Boat

Headship is to be colored by love. Christian leadership is not a dictatorship in either manner or purpose. As Christ leads for the benefit of the church, the husband leads for the benefit of the wife. Headship includes sacrifice *("as Christ loved the church and gave Himself up for her")*. It is dominated by concern for the wife's best *("to make her holy . . . to present her to himself as a radiant church . . . without stain or wrinkle")*. *"Husbands ought to love their wives as their own bodies. (After all, no one ever hated his own body, but he feeds and cares for it, just as Christ does the church)"* (Ephesians 5:25-29).

After reading that, how can a man say, "You want to paint the house blue and I want to paint it green. We'll compromise and paint it green." In the spirit of this passage, how can a husband deny his wife career fulfillment if it is in her best interest and does not interfere with her responsibilities to him and the family? Being led by a husband dominated by love should not in any way deny a woman the liberty and fulfillment she desires.

The Wife's Assignment Not All Homework

Biblical roles do not limit a wife's place to the home. The home is as much the husband's place as the wife's. Some, however, believe God instructed Christian women to stick close to home. Paul's words to Titus are taken as proof for this: *"Teach the older women to be reverent in the way they live . . . then they can train the younger women to love their husbands and children, to be self-controlled and pure, to be busy at home"* (Titus 2:3, 4, 5).

This verse, however, should not be used to shackle women to the kitchen stove. Paul was speaking to a special situation of his day. Younger women tended to be gossipers, running from place to place while neglecting their responsibilities at home. Paul wanted them to handle those duties; he was not telling them that this might be their only work.

In Paul's own tradition, that of the Old Testament, women's work was not limited to housework. The ideal woman described in chapter 31 of the book of Proverbs is involved in other things. She is into real estate, manufacturing, and retailing. She bought land, planted vineyards, sold in the public markets the clothes and other items she made.

This Old Testament picture of a wife being involved in the economic support of the family is typical through history. Before men trotted off to factories, home and economics were closely tied together. Women helped on farms and in cottage industries. Only in modern times has there been this exclusive division of labor between what a man does outside the home and what a women does inside.

A wife can pursue a career and not be disobedient to her scriptural role as long as she fulfills her duty to her family. The same is true of the man. A husband must not allow his work to interfere with his marriage any more than woman should. Both husband and wife have a place in the home. Experts maintain that the absent father may be as damaging as the absent mother.

Neither a woman or a man should believe that work outside the home takes priority over household duties. Caring for each other and for children should take precedence over other pursuits, even those related to church ministries. What seems to have happened to us in recent times is that we have dignified work in society at the expense of the ministry at home. There is nothing wrong in a man or woman discovering fulfillment and worth in a career or job. However, in admitting this, we should not diminish the dignity and importance of being a husband or wife, a father or mother.

There is no reason why a woman should find more worth by climbing poles and fixing wires than she should find in climbing stairs and fixing meals. Though the hand that rocks the cradle can also be found doing other things, this should not have led us to devalue the influence of a wife and mother. This is a cultural condition that Christians can resist.

Submission Is Not Spelled S-I-L-E-N-C-E

A submissive wife can still claim her rights and speak her mind when it is appropriate. Yet one woman gives an account of how she and her friends thought submission was equal to silence.

> We began to take all of the Scriptures regarding women in the most literal sense. Some of the women began wearing head-covers to indicate their submissiveness. We were instructed to deliberately stifle the gifts of the Holy Spirit which we had always practiced in church, so that our husbands would be forced to take a more active role. It was constantly emphasized how important the leadership of men was—since Eve had been deceived, our sex was forever unfit for any kind of decision-making or administration.
>
> Here and there you would hear of a woman having a time of her "rebellion." For instance, a friend of mine had a very difficult childbirth with complications. This, she told me, was God's punishment for having been unsubmissive. When her husband recommended she have a tubal ligation, she felt she dare not disagree. Though tears streamed down her face all the way to the hospital, the operation was performed. Later, she fell into a deep depression and lost all her sexual feelings. When she spoke to the pastor about these problems he advised her to fake it.[8]

The attitude of these women toward submission failed to take into account all of the biblical data.

The woman who submitted to a tubal ligation had the mistaken notion that she should not disagree with her husband. Yet one of the most prominent biblical examples of a meek and quiet wife shows this is not so. Sarah complained to her husband about her servant, Hagar, and the son she had borne to Abraham. Yet Peter still urges women to follow her example as an obedient wife.

A wife is entitled to speak up whenever her rights are involved. In the case of Sarah, her society gave her the right to control her servant, Hagar. But she knew she must have Abraham's word before anything was done. So she brought the matter up. On one occasion, Abraham was greatly distressed about her demand. After he had prayed God said to him: *"Listen to whatever Sarah tells you"* (Genesis 21:8-13).

A woman also has a responsibility to resist her husband if the matter is a moral or spiritual one. Paul does say wives should submit in everything (Ephesians 5:24). But the term "everything" obviously cannot refer to some matters. A wife should not commit adultery in obedience to her husband. A husband cannot tell his wife how to vote.

Matters of personal conscience are not included in the statement *"in everything"* since we are ethically obligated to obey God rather than men (Acts 5:29). When Paul uses the term *everything* he uses it in a limited way. Whenever your partner comes home from the supermarket, you may ask, "Did you buy everything?" Obviously, you don't expect to see trucks lined up on your street ready to unload the whole market. You mean "everything" he went for. When Paul says wives are to submit to their husbands in everything, he refers to those legitimate areas of married life.

A sensitive husband will want to know his wife's viewpoints and feelings before making a final serious decision. The husband who pressured his wife into a tubal ligation should have been open to her arguments and deep emotional resistance. She should have shared this with him, opposing and postponing the decision in order to consider it more carefully.

Submission Is Not Exclusion

Recognizing her husband's leadership does not demand a woman store her abilities on a shelf. His headship does not prevent him from consulting his wife about a decision and even admitting that her intelligence and decision-making ability might be superior. When God designated him as leader, He didn't promise to whisper in his ear or otherwise tell him in some supernatural way what decisions to make. The Christian leader gets all the facts, considers them, and prayerfully decides. A man's wife may be very helpful to him in this area.

Practically, too, headship doesn't demand all decisions be brought to the husband. It would seem that those of the egalitarian position think traditional roles require this. In their eyes there are many practical advantages of the equal marriage viewpoint.

> Minor decisions are made by the person whose area of work or responsibility the decision falls in. If the husband has responsibility for car care, he does not need to consult his wife about the kind of wax or gas he buys or when it is to be washed. She can make suggestions and raise objections during an evaluation session, or at any other time for that matter, but minor choices are his to decide. The same would hold true for any other area. This frees both partners from a lot of needless disagreements.[9]

For many years, I have seen countless couples operate in that same manner, though they still believed in the husband's headship. They still held to the concept that if they disagreed on a major matter, the husband would make the final decision.

Submission need not dictate the wife never take the initiative. Even in the delicate area of sex, she can sometimes become the seeker, the aggressor. It is only when she becomes excessively or thoughtlessly aggressive that she can in some cases cause problems for her husband. Some men have difficulty handling this. But he can be thoughtlessly too aggressive as well. Taking the initiative in this area is not wrong for either person; but doing it in the wrong way might be.

Submission, Not Seizure

Headship cannot be seized by a husband. He can only assume the role if the wife is willing to obey. The New Testament tells the Christian wife to submit to her head. The wife does this as unto the Lord. Allegiance to her commitment to Christ and His plan makes her yielding possible.

This rules out any harsh treatment of a wife who won't comply. A Christian husband is never justified in using abuse, physical or verbal, "to bring his wife into line." If she doesn't submit to his leadership, he is commanded to love her, not lash out at her.

I have often seen evangelical Christian men offended and angry whenever their wives did not play the submissive role as they thought they should. I have already written about one man who was enraged by his wife's housecleaning performance. He considered it insubordination and was so angered he feared he would hurt her physically.

His anger was probably rooted in his disappointment. Being a serious-minded Christian, he was discouraged that his wife did not want to obey God by obeying him. He was not really attacking her housekeeping; he was attacking her spirituality.

In some cases, it is the wife who attacks and pressures the husband for his failure to play his role. Women become bitterly critical whenever they think the husband has let them down.

These reactions are not called for. Forcing partners to comply to biblical roles is not the proper reaction to his/her failure to do so. Paul commands husbands to love their wives, submissive or not, just as Peter commands wives to submit to their husbands, Christian or not.

I believe that the unloving responses are often prompted by too great an emphasis some people place on roles in marriage. The next section will clarify what I mean by this.

Role Your Way to Marital Success?

The headship-submission arrangement is not a cure-all for marriages. In my opinion, some traditional role advocates go beyond what the Bible claims for roles. They seem to say that lack of male leadership is the core of all family problems. Extremists sometimes even extend this beyond the home to society. The key to the kingdom is in the husband's pocket; he must learn to lead, they say.

In the New Testament, God's blessing and marital success are linked to something besides role keeping. When Peter warns that a couple's prayers can be hindered, he doesn't link it to the failure to lead, but the failure to love. *"Husbands,"* he writes, *"in the same*

*way be considerate as you live with your wives, and treat them
with respect as the weaker partner and as heirs with you of the
gracious gift of life, so that nothing will hinder your prayers"* (1 Peter
3:7). Lack of consideration or understanding and lack of respect
are what damage spiritual and marital life.

Our pride, selfishness, and unkindness lead us to misuse our
roles and hurt the relationship. Roles must be coupled with love to
make them effective.

This is why egalitarians do not have the final answer, either.
Giving each other equal power will not instantly transport a couple
to fairyland. Egalitarians can end up hassling, badgering, competing
with, and eventually hating each other, just as those who misuse
the traditional role arrangement.

Either position may have a peaceful relationship without a
satisfying one. Though couples live in harmony in a democratic
relationship or in a headship-submission one, they may have little
of the closeness and understanding that is the essence of the "one
flesh" affair.

The bottom line of the New Testament recipe for marriage is:
Love one another. Couples should not expect a good marriage to
be a place of perfectly executed roles; but they should try to make
it, above all, a place of love.

The Script Calls for Both Roles and Intimacy

Once we see the importance of love, there is no reason why
roles and intimacy cannot go together. The claim that roles prevent
husbands and wives from relating to each other is not true, even
though some would point to the benefits of egalitarian marriage to
support this.

> They are free to share their thoughts and feelings, dreams
> and problems with each other knowing it is all right to be
> what they are. This leads to a personal intimacy far beyond
> that which is possible in a marriage when both are trying
> to be someone they are not. For how can I love the real
> you when you are trying so hard to be someone else.
> And how can you love the real me when I am trying to be
> someone else. They are two lonely people playing games
> with each other, but never really touching souls. [10]

I would agree that some people have elevated marriage based upon roles above one based on closeness and love. Early European immigrants tended to view marriage as an institutional arrangement, not an intimate one.

Roles need not interfere with intimacy, as egalitarians claim. The fault of the past institutional approach lay more in its neglecting intimacy than its designating roles. Couples I know today have both, just as the Bible prescribes. When we accept a certain role in the marriage, we can still be our real selves in our struggle to be our ideal selves. A husband can share with his wife the insecurities he feels; as leader he need not always hide behind a hypocritical mask of strength. A wife can confide in her husband that she has struggles in her effort to be a godly wife.

Instead of preventing it, acceptance of God-assigned roles can provide a harmonious context where intimacy can flourish.

Commune Occasion

Exchanging Expectations: "Tell It Like It Is to Be"

Step One: Read out loud the following passage of Scripture which is the major passage dealing with the roles of husband and wife in marriage.

Submit to one another out of reverence for Christ. Wives, submit to your husbands as to the Lord. For the husband is the head of the wife as Christ is the head of the church, his body, of which he is the Savior. Now as the church submits to Christ, so also wives should submit to their husbands in everything.

Husbands, love your wives, just as Christ loved the church and gave himself up for her to make her holy, cleansing her by the washing with water through the word, and to present her to himself as a radiant church, without stain or wrinkle or any other blemish, but holy and blameless. In this same way, husbands ought to love their wives as their own bodies. He who loves his wife loves himself. After all, no one ever hated his own body, but he feeds and cares for it, just as Christ does the church—for we are members of his body. "For this reason a man will leave his father and mother and be united to his wife, and the two will become one flesh." This is a

profound mystery—but I am talking about Christ and the church.
However, each one of you also must love his wife as he loves himself,
and the wife must respect her husband.　　　(Ephesians 5:21-33)

Step Two: Each of you make a list.
1. The wife lists exactly what she would expect from a husband who followed the suggestions of this passage. Try to be practical and specific.
2. The husband lists exactly what he would expect from a wife who followed the suggestions of this passage. Try to be practical and specific.

Step Three: Beginning with the wife, each of you share your list and then discuss how you will work out your roles in marriage.

ENDNOTES

[1]Cathleen McGuigan, "Newsmakers," *Newsweek,* July 13, 1981, p. 47. Copyright 1981 by Newsweek Inc. All rights reserved. Reprinted by permission.

[2]Patricia Gundry, *Heirs Together: Biblical Equality in Marriage* (Grand Rapids: Zondervan Publishing House, 1978), pp. 22-23.

[3]Ibid., p. 103.

[4]Lou Beardsley and Toni Spry, *The Fulfilled Woman,* p. 23, quoted in Gundry, *Heirs Together: Biblical Equality in Marriage,* p. 21.

[5]Vern L. Bullough and Bonnie Bullough, *The Subordinate Sex* (New York: Penguin Books, Inc., 1974), p. 174.

[6]Ibid., p. 174.

[7]David Gelman with Janet Huck, Eloise Salholzun, Sylvester Monroe, Diane Weathers, Holly Morris, "How Marriages Can Last," *Newsweek,* July 13, 1981, p. 76. Copyright 1981 by Newsweek Inc. All rights reserved. Reprinted by permission.

[8]Erica Diamond, "A Fascinating Woman Gets Sprung or If Marabel Morgan Could Only See Me Now," *Free Indeed,* p. 11, quoted in Gundry, *Heirs Together: Biblical Equality in Marriage,* p. 22.

[9]Gundry, *Heirs Together: Biblical Equality in Marriage,* p. 139.

[10]Ibid., p. 137.

CHAPTER FOURTEEN

WHEN THE CRUNCH COMES
FACING LIFE'S CRISES TOGETHER

Many people think that the rocks on which most marriages flounder are found in the mattress. Some who study marriage disagree. Though adjusting to each other sexually is complex and problematic, there are other adjustments that may be just as tough. One of these is the adjustment to life's crises. Whether small or large these constantly beat upon us like the storm in Jesus' parable. *"The rain came down, and the streams rose, and the winds blew and beat against that house . . . "* He said (Matthew 7:25). Though Jesus is not referring to literal homes, His parable is still an apt description of ordinary family life.

Different Jolts for Different Folks

When these crises occur, they become different things to different marriages. A crisis can be like a battering ram to some, forcing the relationship to near collapse. When such changes and difficulties place stress on us as individuals, they also place a lot of strain on the relationship. A wife's mother dies; an excessive and prolonged grief reaction makes the stricken wife withdraw, become depressed. At first her husband tries to console. Then he gets impatient and harsh as the months drag on. Frequent quarrels drive them further apart. He resents her failure to get help and

"snap out of it." Her sexual unresponsiveness offers them little or
no physical closeness. The personal crisis has now become a marital
one.

At times, a crisis acts like an electronic amplifier. Just like a
public address system can bring a whisper to a deafening roar, a
crisis can bring out and magnify the best and the worst in us. It can
exaggerate a problem in a relationship or enlarge a personal fault.

With the horrible memories of her accident still creating panic
inside her, a woman picked up the phone beside her hospital bed
to call her husband. Holding the phone to her ear as the rings began,
she uncontrollably recalled to herself the crunch of her car slamming
into the other, the dazed confusion, the sound of sirens, the anxious
ride in the ambulance; all of this blended into her present relief that
she was not seriously injured. Anxious to tell her husband all of
this, to receive some emotional strength from him, she was comforted
by the familiar "Hello" that came through the receiver. Hurriedly
she said, "I've been in a car accident."

But before she could say more, he interrupted her sternly,
"How much damage did you do to the car?" Previously she had
been dismayed by his seeming unconcern for her, his taking her for
granted. Now his immediate worry was not for her, but for the car.
Once the husband learned she was calling from a hospital bed, he
knew it would be a long time before he could ever live down those
few words he could never take back. As Ginger and I look back
over our years of marriage, we have seen this effect of crises on us.
The most damaging things we have ever said to each other have
been during some stressful experience.

But a crisis can be like glue. Troubles can strengthen the bond
between you. For this reason, the authors of a book on marital
intimacy include crisis intimacy as one of the most important kinds.
Being in a stew is no fun, but it can blend the two of you together.
A fearful wife feels the reassuring grip of her husband's hand as she
is being wheeled into the operating area. A husband is held in his
wife's tight embrace after reporting to her he has just lost his job.
Tears of grief may be just as binding as touches of love.

Ready for Anything

Whether a crisis will strengthen or strain a relationship will
depend upon how it is handled. This is one reason why we should

be as prepared as possible to meet these crises, whether they are tragic or trivial.

Not that we can ever be completely prepared. They always seem to hit us on the blind side. When one comes, we usually greet it with the words, "If only it would have been something else; I was prepared for other things, but not for this." Probably we say this because it is not really possible to be fully prepared for any kind of trouble. We can read about troubles, but reading is not the same as enduring. Even going through a personal struggle with him/her is not nearly equivalent to going through it ourselves. Yet we can do some things to get ready for whatever comes.

Recently Billy Graham wrote a book on how to prepare for a future catastrophe: Armageddon. But he was not only writing about this future day of doom. In his own words he says: "That's what my book was about—how to prepare both for the great Armageddon that will come some day and for the little 'armageddons' we each face in our own lives. . . . Each of us faces problems—an illness, a family problem, an economic reversal—and we need to prepare for those times now."[1] Good marriage preparation includes preparing for these little armageddons.

Getting ready begins in your head: cultivating the right thoughts and attitudes toward problems and suffering. It is the spiritual stance toward these matters that will influence you most. Jesus said that the house that can stand the storm is built upon His Word. Here the Christian has an advantage. Our faith provides answers about human suffering. The Apostle Paul had one of the boldest postures toward life's hardships. *"I am ready for anything through the strength of the One who lives within me"* (Philippians 4:13, Phillips).

Paul's attitude couldn't be described as either pessimistic or optimistic. He knew tough times would come. He didn't optimistically convince himself they wouldn't. Nor was pessimism producing morbid thoughts of future tragedies, smothering his joy in Christ. Trusting in Christ, Paul was neither sadly pessimistic nor blindly optimistic; he was just ready.

Discipline Is for Legitimate Kids

Paul's readiness and ours will be based on a proper **u**nderstanding of the reason for human suffering. While Christians **are** not left without suffering, they are not left without an explanation of it.

In one of the prominent passages on Christian suffering, the author of Hebrews labels the Christian life struggles as *"the chastening of the Lord"* (Hebrews 12:5, KJV). Chastening refers to the kind of training parents do. The passage tells us God, like a father, trains His children through suffering.

None of His children are exempt. This is the opposite of what Christians sometimes believe. Being a Christian doesn't free you from trouble, it promises it to you. *"Endure hardship as discipline; God is treating you as sons. For what son is not disciplined by his father? If you are not disciplined (and everyone undergoes discipline), then you are illegitimate children and not true sons"* (Hebrews 12:7, 8). Being a child of God makes you subject to suffering, not free from it. Billy Graham says, "I do not agree with those who say our lives should be trouble free if we are following Christ."[2]

Not expecting trouble is the best way to be unprepared for it. Then it really hits hard, and hurts more. A period of time as a hospital chaplain made this clear to me. The Christians who had the most difficulty with sickness were those who believed they were above such a thing. They usually were not only physically ill, they were emotionally depressed.

I recall one extreme case of this. When I entered the hospital room, I sensed something more than physical was wrong. The look on the woman's face was one of despair. She was polluting the atmosphere with gloom. When I asked about her sadness she explained she was facing surgery in the morning. I had just talked with several patients who faced even more serious surgery than she; their emotions were not so shattered. She continued, "I have been putting off surgery because the people of my church and I have been praying for healing. But it has not come; now the doctor says the operation cannot be delayed. Since God has not healed me, I assume I must not be one of His children."

How I empathized for this woman who not only felt sick, but felt forsaken. I tried, without success, to explain the message of Hebrews 12. Healing was not necessary to confirm she was a child of God. God deals with us as His children. He will put us into difficulties to try our faith, to shape us. This is not a threat to us; it is a promise. He will not permit us to get far out of His will. He will bring us into line through the discipline of circumstance.

When the Crunch Comes

Discipline Is a Sign of Love

He does not do this because He hates us or because He wants to destroy. *"Whom the Lord loves, He chastens."* Chastening displays His love, not his anger. He judges unbelievers in anger; but He graciously disciplines Christians in love. Paul explains, *"We are being disciplined (by the Lord) so that we will not be condemned with the world"* (1 Corinthians 11:32).

God's discipline is accomplished by allowing hard circumstances to come to us. For the Hebrews it came in the form of persecution by nonbelievers. They were being ostracized from nonbelieving Jews, probably excommunicated from the synagogue and prevented from doing business in the community. This suffering, however, is still called God's training. Seeing God's love behind our trials will cast them in a different and revolutionary light.

Imagine the application of this truth: Whom the Lord loves He chastens. A wife enters the door of the home. Moments before she had seen her doctor who has arranged for her to enter the hospital for important tests. Stepping through the door, she calls to her husband, "Honey, come here; I want to tell you how God has expressed His love to us today." Or imagine a husband at the kitchen table, opening the morning mail. His eyes fall on a bill which is several hundred dollars more than he expected. Fighting anger and discouragement, he says to himself: "Well Lord, I wondered how You were going to show me Your love today."

Discipline Is Not to Be Interpreted in Extremes

Receiving such hardships as signs of God's love should not lead us to certain extremes in accepting them. Some speakers and writers suggest we should welcome adversity to the point that we are able to thank God for everything. But accepting life's tragedies need not include being thankful for them. Christians should be able to accept evil and thank God that *"in all things God works for the good of those who love him"* (Romans 8:28). We are not counseled to be grateful for evil. It is a perverted and distorted mind that encourages us to thank God for the death of a young child or the rape of a sister. Though Paul says we should be able in everything to give thanks, this cannot mean we must be thankful for everything that happens to us.

There is another dangerous extreme to avoid when facing a

crisis: trying to see some particular sin lurking behind it. It is true that God's training is sometimes a form of spanking. Yet the word "discipline" refers to more than God's woodshed activities. Not every crisis is a punishment for sin. It is true that human suffering in general comes from the fact that mankind has sinned. But not every particular adversity is caused by a particular shortcoming. God may bring something tough our way just to stretch us and make us grow. Even so there are lots of Christians around who want to pin the blame on themselves or others for every negative thing that comes along.

Searching for the misdeed behind the misery can be particularly damaging to a marriage relationship. Always asking, "Why did this happen to us?" may generate a general sense of guilt that hinders you from facing the problem. Or else individuals inwardly or outwardly begin to lay blame on one another. Certainly it may be a good idea to do some introspective soul searching when you have a setback of some sort. Suffering is partly designed to make us walk straighter paths. *"No discipline seems pleasant at the time, but painful. Later on, however, it produces a harvest of righteousness and peace* (Hebrews 12:11).

Examine yourself when you're in a crisis, but be careful not to overdo it. However, you need also to concentrate on looking ahead, not just backward. People who get caught up in blaming themselves or someone else are lulled into inactivity at a time when they may most of all need to act. A problem is to solve or get through. If we are occupied with the judgment of ourselves and others, we may lose the good judgment we need.

Discipline Is for Growth

Realizing that the ultimate purpose of discipline is our growth will foster a positive attitude toward it. Growing in grace is the most important process in the Christian life. Being successful, being useful, being healthy, being happy are all secondary to being conformed to the image of Christ. This is why God will use failure, illness, and unhappiness to achieve His greater purpose. Otherwise, when these things come, they will make us think God hates us, has forsaken us, or just plain condemns us. That is not the message trouble is designed to bring.

Having endured a Nazi concentration camp, watching indescribable suffering, the psychologist Victor Frankl concluded that anything that doesn't kill us can be good for us. Though I have never seen the suffering Victor Frankl has, I have seen people who confirmed his words. I heard an unbelievable comment from a terminally ill young husband and father that suggests anything can offer some good to us. I was sitting with him by a lake on a brilliant summer day at a men's retreat. We had just come from the cabin where I had seen him grimace in pain as he injected a hypodermic full of chemical into the plastic tube that protruded through a hole in his abdomen. These daily doses of chemical were part of the only possible treatment left to save him from the cancer that was taking his life. It was because of him that the men of his church and I were at that camp at that time. Fearing he might not live another month, the committee asked that the date be changed so they could have one final retreat together. The occasion was an unusual blend of love and sadness.

Looking down on the healthy, active men below churning up the lake with their noisy horseplay, I felt free to challenge my sick friend to be honest with me. He had just told me that his illness was the best thing that had ever happened to him. "Are you sure?" I asked. "I have heard people talk like that; but, without your being pious, without trying to kid me, tell me if you really mean that statement."

His genuine smile seemed to temporarily bring a flush of health to his pallid face. "These last two years have been the best two years of my life," he said with unmistakable conviction. Then he told me about the beautiful relationship he and his wife had developed, how he had been able to spend so many happy hours with his three-year-old boy. Because of cancer, he had experienced a quality of life he never before thought possible. When someone phoned me of his death two weeks later, I thanked God that He could turn such suffering into growth.

An Approach for All Crises

Life's crises do not always come with the big labels: death, accident, terminal illness. The difficulties that plague us the most are sometimes the little ones. When we think of being prepared for crises, we must not think of the once-in-a-lifetime tragedies, but the everyday problems. Like little termites can fell the biggest oak, little daily problems can eat away at us and our relationship. How we handle these in the long run may determine the success of our marriage relationship. Successfully facing little problems will be the best preparation for facing the big ones.

Pray about Everything, Worry about Nothing

Perhaps this concern for everyday struggles is behind Paul's advice on how to face anxiety: *"Do not be anxious about anything, but in everything, by prayer and petition, with thanksgiving, present your requests to God"* (Philippians 4:6). Pray about everything, Paul said, not just the big things. Commenting on the passage, one speaker said: "Pray about everything and worry about nothing. Or pray about nothing and worry about everything."

Get used to regularly coming to God about the things that bug you. If you do it about the small things, it will sort of develop a habit whenever something more major occurs.

Praying is only the beginning of problem solving.

Faith It

Whatever the problem, it will usually not get solved if we don't face it. Too often we deny problems or ignore them, thinking they will just dissolve like the morning fog. Doctors tell us of cancer patients who ignore symptoms until it is too late to treat the illness. Psychologists tell us of married couples who put off seeking help for a problem until it has grown to gigantic and complicated proportions.

Being a Christian gives us faith to face our problems, not to pretend they are not there. Malcom Jones, a man who found himself in a tragic situation, tells us how he learned to do this. The single engine plane in which he had been riding crashed in the middle of the Florida Everglades. Bent over in the seat next to him, the pilot was bleeding badly. The flow of blood told Jones there was not much time to get help for his friend. He started wading through the swamp in the direction of a nearby town. After a hundred feet or so of water and mud, sometimes up to his waist, he was gripped by fear of what he saw before him. In the moonlight he could see two huge glistening eyes in the water. He could hear the loud bellowing and splashing of the angry jaws of a female alligator. Beside her were pairs of smaller eyes signaling to Jones that he was standing in the middle of her nest.

At that moment he recalled the advice of the oldtimers of the region: "Never walk into an alligator nest." He also thought of some words, as if a voice spoke to him: "I am with you always." Taking that promise of His Lord, Malcom Jones walked straight ahead muttering, "Momma, I am not going to hurt you or your children; I have to go for help for my friend." The clapping of her jaws got fiercer and her tail slapped the water as he came near. But, finally, the huge pair of eyes moved off to the left, followed by a line of smaller ones.

Jones said that before he was out of the swamp he had, in the same way, walked through a dozen or more alligator nests. After his friend was rescued and the ordeal was over, he said he received a lesson about life: "Face your problems; don't retreat from them."

Retreat is all too common. A husband and wife don't adjust well sexually. Yet they put off getting help, finding a solution, too embarrassed or too proud to admit they need help. Personal problems, too, get swept under the rug: we ignore the symptoms of overeating, hot tempers, depression, overworking, etc.

Allow the Proper Owner to Own It

When facing a problem, each of you will need to see your relationship to it. People who study problem solving tell us one of the important questions to ask is, "Who owns the problem?" They caution us about trying to solve someone else's personal problem for them.

For instance, a wife who cannot control her eating may ask her husband to curb her appetite for her. If he accepts the responsibility for her behavior, she will not feel responsible herself. This makes the problem less solvable since it is much easier to solve your own problems than to solve someone else's. And the problem may soon interfere with the relationship. He cautions her every time she reaches for a dessert. This soon turns into nagging, angry looks, and harsh words. She sneaks something out of the refrigerator when he is not around. His suspicions are aroused and their trust for one another deteriorates.

What a husband should do in such a situation is to say, "Sorry, I cannot accept this responsibility. It is your problem; you and the Lord must solve it together. I will support, encourage, and pray for you. Let me know how I can help, but don't make me responsible for controlling what I can't." Husbands and wives can too easily become dependent upon one another in the wrong way. The result is that problems don't get solved and the relationship is under a heavy stress.

The person who lives with someone with a personal struggle is not entirely separated from it. Yet he does not have the same problem as his spouse. If a woman lives with a man who has a quick, angry temper, her problem is not his quick temper. Her problem is learning how to live with a man who has such a temper. She must successfully adapt herself to his temperament while he learns, by God's grace, to control it.

Watch for the Fallout

Recognizing how our problems affect one another is also very important to problem solving. Whenever a crisis or personal struggle takes place, there is a fallout. Everyone who is closely related is affected. And so we must learn to deal with everyone involved. If a husband and wife constantly quarrel, it creates a problem for the children in the family. While they learn to do better at settling their differences, they must also help the child handle the problems caused by their quarreling. A child may feel guilty, thinking he is the cause of the parents' fights. Or else he may feel ashamed, especially if he knows the neighbors hear his parents quarrel.

For this reason, a death of a close friend or relative will cause numerous reactions within a family. The mother's grief may generate anger that makes her lash out at the children. Or a child may inwardly grieve at the death of a grandparent in such a way that it is not noticed by the grieving parents. Parents may misunderstand the symptoms, poor school grades or angry outbursts, and fail to support the child. Because of this type of fallout we should be alert to everyone's reactions to troubles.

Managing the Big "G" and the Common "D"

Two of the most common reactions to stressful situations demand some special understanding. Understanding how to cope with these will put a Christian in a good place to face life's common distresses.

Grappling with Grief

Grief is something Christians and non-Christians experience frequently. When the Apostle Paul said that Christians would not grieve as those who have no hope, he was not saying we do not have grief, just that we don't have the hopeless grief of the non-believer. The rest of the New Testament confirms this. Paul himself was not ashamed to say God had spared him *"sorrow upon sorrow,"* by healing his friend (Philippians 2:27). *"Sorrow upon sorrow"* is a Greek phrase that refers to deep, intense grief. Paul also accepted grief when other Christians experienced it. He didn't rebuke the Ephesian Christians for weeping aloud and grieving because it was the last time they would see him (Acts 20:37-38).

Modern studies of grief show that it is not just a reaction to death. Apparently, we have a grief reaction to any important loss: when we lose a friend, lose or change jobs, move to another city, etc.

When grief occurs, it is best not to deny it or resist it too much. It is good to force yourself to participate in life's activities, putting yourself in circumstances that will lift your spirits. But it is not healthy to pretend the sadness is not there or to blame yourself for not being able to snap out of it at will. When your partner grieves, you must also resist blaming them or forcing them to deny what is really there.

It will help if you know just how grief behaves. We know that there are several stages it goes through. Obviously, the severity and length of each stage will vary according to the nature of the loss and the temperament of the individual.

Stage One: Shock. Denial and disbelief accompany an emotional or physical feeling of shock. Perhaps feelings and expressions of anger also appear. If someone says bitter things about the doctor when his or her mother dies, we don't take such accusations seriously and scold or argue. When the emotions subside, a reasonable perspective will be restored.

Stage Two: Controlled Rage. Much of the individual's attention and energy goes toward controlling the disappointment and anger within. A person will become passive, perhaps be slow of reaction, have a feeling of emptiness. In extreme forms, they may come to the verge of a psychic breakdown where they feel they are "going crazy." Fear, panic, and anxiety may grip them. They need someone near who can reassure them they are normal and that it will pass.

Stage Three: Regressive.   During this stage the person is trying to cope with the loss. It may not appear to be too constructive or rational. The griever may feel helpless and tense or even apathetic, having a difficult time keeping interest in his or her job or other duties. He may have less self-respect and criticize himself a lot. Communication with God may be more difficult because of the deep feelings of anger toward Him. He or she may be fighting guilt, anxiety, anger, and depression.

Stage Four: Adaption.   Now more constructive forms of handling the loss replace the negative ones. If angry outbursts, for example, were part of stage three, the griever in this stage may get back to jogging or playing tennis. Or resentful thoughts about God are replaced with new awareness of His wisdom in knowing what is best. The person may suddenly feel liberated, now no longer looking on himself or herself as a "mourner." The lost person, job, or place is not forgotten. Instead there is a new attitude toward what was lost.

The person can now emotionally handle the fact that the person or thing is gone; but it is still in some sense restored. Whereas before, the widow could not think of her lost husband without intense inner pain, she can now remember him and their life together with satisfaction. She has adjusted to the loss of his presence on the one hand, but has found him once again, in another way: this time in her memories. The lost person is thrust aside, yet restored.

This final positive stage could not be arrived at without the other stages of struggle. One writer calls the whole process "good grief," meaning that we must encourage ourselves and others to go successfully through the experience. Though we won't be able to control all our inner feelings, we can manage our actions, not allowing our grief to drive us to do harmful things: getting rid of our anger by lashing out at those close to us; allowing feelings of resentment to renounce your faith in God's love. Rather, we should understand that the anger, resentment, depression are temporary; they will pass. In the meantime, we must continue to function as wisely as possible.

A griever's experience may be abnormal if it is prolonged at any one stage. If, for example, a man continues to deny his wife's death two or three months after it has occurred, he will need some professional help. Or abnormalities occur whenever the means of coping with the loss indicate the person has not been fully accepting. A Chicago man, for example, still keeps his son's room as it was when the boy died more than ten years ago. He goes into the room regularly and looks at and handles the clothes and toys and other mementoes of his son's existence. The man has never adjusted fully to the loss. He wants to continue the relationship now denied him instead of accepting the loss and moving on with his own life.

Dealing with Depression

Depression is common today. Popular terms like "being down" and in "the pits," remind us how preoccupied we are with blue moods. One counselor friend of mine says that half of all his patients come because they are depressed. It is the most common kind of abnormal behavior according to the experts. Since each of us has a one in ten chance of becoming severely depressed, we ought to be acquainted with it.

When you're depressed, life seems worthless. Feelings of helplessness, worthlessness, and a loss of self-esteem close in on you. Pessimism blots out the future and a terrible sadness sets in. Outwardly, the depressed person loses interest in ordinary life events, and complains that doing simple tasks is like climbing a cliff. Varieties of symptoms crop up: poor concentration, headaches, chest pains, and lack of sex drive.

Psychologists tell us that they still don't understand depression well enough to break it down into types. But for practical reasons, it is possible to distinguish two different kinds. Normal depression is something we all have from time to time. We feel a lack of energy and maybe an extra heavy dose of being down on ourselves. It's tough to get up in the A.M. and we don't feel like starting the day; and even if we did, we don't feel worthy enough to contribute much.

All of these symptoms are the same as in more severe forms of depression; but there are differences. First, you can usually point to a cause: a recovering from illness, a period of grieving, tiredness after completing an exhausting project, or the "time of the month." Also, the depressed condition doesn't last long; we may miss a day or so of work, but it would not linger around long enough to incapacitate us. This kind of depression is more regular for some people than others. Some of us have a depressive sort of temperament, and our loved ones learn to accept us and live with it.

When depression is prolonged and interferes with living, it is classified as a more serious type: neurotic depression. For weeks and months, the sufferer feels sad, blue, guilty, deserted, lost, and empty. And all of this is coupled with a loss of hope, believing nothing can be done to help. Rejoicing seems to be impossible whenever a person is in this state.

The Christian's first approach will be to use his spiritual resources. Reading and memorizing Scripture and spending time with the Lord are among the most effective things he can do. But he will also know that these measures will not always lift the gloom. Great spiritual leaders have suffered with the kind of depression that a close walk with God did not immediately cure.

Martin Luther suffered terrible moods and wrote about them: "For more than a week I was close to the gates of death and hell. I trembled in all my members. Christ was wholly lost. I was shaken by desperation. . . ."[3] While Luther relied on God's help, he also tried some down-to-earth cures. He advised people with mild bouts of depression to ignore the heavy head and avoid solitude. Get out where there is music, joking, and the company of others. Manual labor also offers relief. A good way, counseled Luther, to exorcise the Devil was to harness the horse and spread manure on the fields.[4]

Sometimes rest and withdrawal from a stressful situation may be needed. Staying home from the job or taking a short vacation may pull you out. Sometimes you may need to search for the cause. Past events could have generated some hot anger that has transformed itself into feelings of depression. Then you'll need to deal with anger by admitting it to yourself and talking it out with the Lord and others.

Talking with others about your feelings may be the best release for depressive moods. For this reason, husbands and wives are in a crucial spot to help each other. Studies show that people who have a close companion are less likely to become severely depressed.

You can't help a depressed partner by nagging him or her to snap out of it, impatiently employing that "Enough is enough." Counsel them to do something about it and support them in their efforts to handle it. Remember, a depressed person feels down, down upon life and down upon himself. He already has enough criticism and blame. Piling more on him will only make him/her sink lower. Patient, loving understanding will be the best medicine. And we can always remind ourselves and the depressed person of the good news: Depression always eventually goes away.

Ready for the Blessing?

For Christians, a successful marriage will not result from being free of trouble but from being ready for it. There is no victory without a battle, no success without struggle. "We need to realize," Billy Graham suggests, "that God brings great blessing to us through suffering and difficulties."[5]

Commune Occasion

Sharing Our Attitudes

Read out loud this verse and then discuss the questions that follow.

And we know that in all things God works for the good of those who love him, who have been called according to his purpose. Romans 8:28

1. The passage does not say that all things are good. However, do you believe that we will in this life learn why some difficulty, problem, or tragedy has happened by seeing good come out of it?
2. Have you had experiences in the past that confirm this verse?
3. How do you feel about life's sufferings?

Understanding Our Responses

Answer and discuss the following completions.
● Whenever I face some unusually trying difficulty or crisis, I tend to:
   a. Want to be alone.
   b. Go to pieces.
   c. Get very critical.
   d. Draw closer to God.
   e. Get angry with God and others.
   f. Get depressed.

g. Try to escape in recreation or business.

h. Other _____

● Whenever one or both of us faces a crisis, it tends to interfere with our relationship in the following manner:

a. One of us doesn't want to talk.

b. One of us talks too much.

c. We tend to blame each other.

d. We both hurt so much we don't support each other.

e. Our relationship changes in some way that is detrimental.

f. Other _____

Lending Our Support

● Whenever I face a crisis, you can most help me by offering the following:

a. Lending a shoulder to cry on.

b. Being there to talk to.

c. Being present, but not talking about it.

d. Sharing biblical truths and spiritual thoughts that help me think it through.

e. Help me have fun and enjoy life.

f. Pray with me.

g. Other _____

ENDNOTES

[1]"Candid Conversation with the Evangelist," *Christianity Today,* July 17, 1981, p. 23. Copyright 1981 by *Christianity Today.* Used by permission.

[2]Ibid., p. 23.

[3]Roland Bainton, *Here I Stand* (Nashville: Abingdon, 1950), p. 36.

[4]Ibid., p. 364.

[5]"Candid Conversation with the Evangelist," *Christianity Today,* p. 23.

CHAPTER FIFTEEN

"MATRI MONEY" UNDERSTANDING MONEY MATTERS IN MARRIAGE

Money matters. Probably far more than we realize. Jesus called riches "deceitful" (Mark 4:19). And the Apostle Paul claimed that *"the love of money is a root of all kinds of evil"* (1 Timothy 6:10). Wrong attitudes toward money can fool us and plunge us into serious trouble, some of it marital.

There Are Many Layers in the Ball of Wax

Take the case of Jane Pendle. Jane earned more than her husband Herb. Her doing so was no problem; but her constant mentioning of it to her husband was. Jane kept Herb under her thumb by regular reminders that were it not for her, they wouldn't have any meat on the table or shingles over their heads. Despite the two incomes, they were always in debt because Jane bought everything she wanted. She felt she had all those things coming to her. A man who knew the couple explained her impulsive buying as a way of dealing with the lack of care from her husband. Needing some nurturing, she was unconsciously saying to herself, "I can let the credit companies and banks nurture me." With their financial ship sinking, their marriage was on the rocks.

For better or worse, money and marriage are tied together. As one financial adviser says, "If they are scraping, they are usually scrapping." And it works the other way around. Constant quarreling may drive one or the other to debt as a way of compensating for the lack of a healthy relationship.

Understanding money matters begins with seeing how finances are linked to your relationship and how your relationship is tied to finances.

Getting Tangled in the Purse Strings

Your financial outlook will color how you relate to each other. Jane saw her husband as lacking in ability to meet her needs. Earning more than he, she viewed herself as superior. Apparently, this caused him to feel inferior, making him less able to lead, guide, and care for her. His lack of financial care apparently made it hard for him to give emotional support. This relational problem pressed his wife to find an answer. She tried to buy satisfaction and instead got sadness.

Underneath all of this, of course, was Jane's poor orientation to money. She would not have made so much of her husband's lower wage if she had not placed too high a value on money in the first place.

Our personal inadequacies often cause financial difficulties. The financial troubles are like the top layer of the "ball of wax" we've gotten into. Underneath the top layer is greed. Wanting too much, too fast, couples submerge themselves in debt. Strip away the layer of greed and another problem is likely to show up. For example, greed can be caused by a lack of self-esteem. A person wraps things around himself to cover his inferiority complex.

Our society whets our appetites and fosters our personal problems. The world and the flesh ally themselves against us. Advertisers tell us no one feels inferior in a Corvette. And a little plastic credit card gives us recognition and power while acting as the key to the door of happiness.

Even a feeling of superiority (pride, the Bible calls it) can get you into a fiscal pickle. We convince ourselves that nothing is too good for us. And Madison Avenue echoes back to our ego: "You deserve it."

Dr. Raymond Pendleton, a clinical psychologist, observes that different people have different reasons for spending more money than they have. Emotional causes rank high. "Impulsivity is one reason," he explains. "People think, if I don't grab everything now,

I'm going to lose it." Plus, "There is tremendous pressure in our society to be like everyone else. This means buying a new car, new clothes, going out to eat three times a week. You can see it at work in middle-class neighborhoods at Christmas. People spend thousands of dollars on gauche lighting displays trying to outshine their neighbors."[1]

Once the personal problems cause the financial ones, the financial struggle stretches the relationship to the breaking point. It's depressing to live uncomfortably in a snow pile of debts. Guilt and anxiety work on both husband and wife. One or both become crabby. To solve the problems, they work more hours. They see each other less. When they do, both are tired and irritable. Under this kind of pressure, stress develops while the relationship doesn't. Neither their marriage nor their financial situation is ready for a crisis, if it should come. The wife may become pregnant, or one may lose a job. Instead of supporting one another and pulling together, they accuse and blame.

The terrible downward spiral is happening to many couples: Personal inadequacies cause marital conflicts; these combine with our culture's pressure to buy and consume; this leads to financial entanglements and strangle the marriage.

It is not surprising that money problems are listed as a major cause of alienation in half of all divorces. One study has shown that eighty percent of all arguments in the home center around money.[2]

Tied Together with the Purse Strings

Of course there is the other side. A good marriage is linked to finances just as a poor one is connected to them. Couples who have a good relationship can help each other control their spending and live within their means. Even if they make mistakes and debts mount, emotional pressure binds them closer together. Their solid relation "ship" makes it through the financial storms.

Even so there is still plenty of evidence to show that there is no pressure in a marriage like financial pressure. And with little hope that the economic situation in the world will offer us much stability in the near future, it is wise to work together in this area.

"Matri Money" Management

This brief chapter can hardly deal with all you will need to know about finances. You'll learn a lot by talking to a financial counselor or by reading books like those found in the reading list at the end of this book.

Money Talks

Initially, you can benefit by some good discussion about money matters. It's easier to neglect this than we think. Possible problems in our marriages' money matters may be harder to talk about than sexual ones.

Its importance makes me always put this area in pre-marital discussions. One of the hottest premarital sessions I ever had was over finances. I poured kerosene on the fiery dialogue because I knew how crucial it was for this couple to air it. Since both of them were in their late twenties, I knew that their financial attitudes and lifestyles were etched fairly deeply into each of them. If their approaches were quite different, it would signal trouble ahead. Actually, for a couple of this age, neither of whom had previously married, sexual adjustment would probably be less difficult than financial. Neither had any long term sexual experience with another to bring into the relationship. But each was bringing years of habits and experience relating to money.

So I asked them each to explain their ideas on handling family finances. They could not have been more opposite in their approach. "Spend until it runs out," he said with conviction. "That's the way I do it and it always worked for my mother and dad." A bit timid, but with conviction to match his, she said, "I think we should carefully plan a budget and keep track of every cent." They started a discussion that was still going on when they left me. Later, they admitted that up to that point, they had never talked about money management.

Even if you have been married for a while, you may not have discussed this area thoroughly.

Counselor Ann Rogers claims that an amazing number of families operate on rules that have never been verbalized.

I remember a pastor and his wife who were referred to me by a marriage counselor. Their marriage was on the rocks. The problem was that they each had different expectations about what they would do with their finances and they never talked about it. Once they were able to air their expectations with each other they could sit back and look at their financial situation objectively together. I worked with them for six months, and when their financial problems were dealt with, the marriage was healed.[3]

Settling these basic matters will prevent a lot of dollars-and-cents arguments. For example, a husband may believe that hard-earned money is to be spent on well-deserved fun. Therefore, whenever they spend money he wants to give priority to entertainment, whether it's a videodisc player or an evening at the Steak Joynt. But his wife's underlying feeling is that money should be put into lasting things. She presses him to invest in good old antique furniture instead of good old times at the ball park. Because of these underlying differences, couples need to grapple with the following questions.

What Are Your Answers to the Basics?

What do you value most in life? Spiritual things, relating to people, having some financial security, some fun, relaxing recreation, doing things related to nature, working hard, serving others, etc. After making a list, try to put them in order.

How are any of the above things related to finances? For example, a person might want to spend a lot of money in ski equipment and ski trips, or will want to invest a lot in missions or helping with social problems.

How hard are we willing to work for what we value? And you might even ask, "How hard should we work for these priorities?" Many Americans have become servants, working long hours for the benefit of the bank, the finance company, the clothing stores, electronics firms, etc. They may not have thought whether or not they really wanted to be in this situation. You need to ask: "Should we kill ourselves for a new set of living room furniture? Should we fight over department store bills? Why should we mortgage our present and compromise our future for a powerboat?" If you decide to do so, fine. But first, count the cost.

How does money and what we can do with it relate to each of our personalities, desires, dreams? Questions in this category include: "Do I feel guilty spending money without planning? Do I have a dream for something in the future I would really like to work and save for? Do I associate money with power? Do I have a poor self-image if I don't have what the neighbors have?"

What do we think about going into debt? Every personal money management book I've read makes this question as a life or debt issue. Whether writing from a Christian viewpoint or not, economists warn of the dangers of losing the spending battle and becoming mired deep in the debt trap.

Sensible Christian writers realize that mortgages, installment payments, and bank loans are not forbidden by the biblical command to *"Owe nothing to anyone"* (Romans 13:8, NASB). As long as existing debts (what is owed) do not exceed assets (funds used to pay what is owed), this verse of Scripture is not violated. Obviously some so-called modern debts may be considered wise investments. Taking a mortgage to buy a house has been an effective means of accumulating some financial assets while at the same time providing you with necessary living space.

Whenever a person accepts monthly payments he cannot handle, he has incurred debt of the wrong kind. Usually the Christian financial counselors suggest that the debt-asset account be an annual one. Theologian Charles Ryrie says, "A family whose annual budget shows a deficit is in serious trouble."[4]

Questions related to your discussion of debt should include those that deal with your emotions and personality. How do you feel about having debts? Do they cause you excessive worry? Does a credit card or charge account make it too easy for you to spend? Do you tend to rely too heavily on debt as a way of getting what you want? "Unbiblical debt is like alcoholism," says Ryrie. "It begins with a little bit the person thinks he can handle. Then a little more . . . and soon the individual is hooked."[5]

Though you probably won't agree on your answers to the basic questions, you will at least know where each stands. With that awareness, you will have a much better chance of attaining harmony in your future financial discussions and dealings.

Who Is in Charge Here?

Though you may have already answered this question, you should think carefully about who will handle the "matri money." Christian couples may tend to answer quickly: The husband should handle it.

Is this wise? I think it is biblically clear that the husband, as home leader, should be ultimately responsible for financial decisions.

But it is probably unwise for him to struggle in his own little corner over money matters without involving his wife and children. Financial experts tell us that the whole family needs to be included in the monetary goings on. George Ford, writing to evangelical Christians, advises, "Some men think they should take care of all the financial matters of the family. Others are willing to leave it to their wives. Neither way is right; finances should be a family affair, involving husband, wife and children who are old enough to participate."[6]

Communication between family members will help everyone know what you are planning to do with your money and why. A family-wise man will want his wife and children to be money-wise. That won't happen if he merely asks them to rubber-stamp his decisions even if he has made them carefully. If all of the family has thought through the decision to trim the spending in order to save for the summer trek to the mountains, he'll have less hassle about the temporary sacrifices involved. Besides—having everyone involved in financial matters forces everyone to keep learning about and grappling with questions of values. As financial leader, the husband will want to get his whole family thinking about earning, giving, and spending.

How Do You Spell Relief from Financial Woe? B-U-D-G-E-T

No one has invented anything better than a budget for managing money. But a budget is a dreaded word we'd like to avoid. "Isn't budgeting a type of slavery?" For most of us, choosing not to follow a budget is equivalent to choosing to follow our impulses. And being enslaved to our desires is servanthood of the worst kind. According to Scripture we are all prone to the insidious voice of covetousness: "I must have this; I can't live without that." Greeds of this kind must be controlled by the Holy Spirit within us. And the best practical bridle for our excessive cravings is a budget.

Many articles and books offer steps for budgeting your spending. They are simple to understand but not easy to follow. Budgeting takes hard work. You must keep accurate records. George Ford says that most of us should spend up to fifteen hours a month keeping an eye on our finances. When people ask him how to find the time to do it, he tells them, "Use some of your worry time."[7]

Ann Rogers has one of the most succinct set of guidelines for budgeting.

Step 1. Prayer. "This is very important," says Vendt. "Since we're in the business of managing God's wealth, we'd better check in with the Master and give ourselves to him as part of our spiritual worship."

Step 2. Set goals. Goals might include buying a new car, giving money to the poor, getting out of debt or starting to save money. "Remember," says Vendt, "a goal is determined by a time frame. You don't just say, 'I want to increase my giving by 10 percent in the next six months.' You need the time frame so you can check yourself. Always be specific about how much money you plan to set aside per week or month and for what purpose."

Step 3. Determine your net worth. This is done by listing your assets (your money in the bank and possessions) against your liabilities (the money you owe to others). The difference between your assets and liabilities is your net worth.

Step 4. Determine your net income. This is your spendable income—the money in your paycheck after all the taxes are taken out.

Step 5. Determine your expenses. This may take awhile to figure out if you haven't been keeping careful track. Don't leave anything out.

Step 6. Evaluation. Put your expenses against your income and determine how to balance the two.

Step 7. Set priorities. This ties back into the goals set in step two. Without unlimited resources, you can't have unlimited goals. You need to choose which goals are most urgent and which can wait until next year or the year after.

Step 8. Execution. The most brilliantly balanced budget will not work unless the plans are faithfully carried out. "This whole process," says Vendt, "must be braced with communication and discipline."[8]

One of the ways to maintain some pocketbook discipline is to keep reminding yourself of the benefits of managing your money instead of being managed by it. By staying out of debt instead of being heavily indebted, you can increase your giving and living by 25 percent, according to one financial advisor.[9] And Ryrie mentions the spiritual profits: "Scripture has been obeyed, giving to the Lord's work enhanced, contentment learned and tensions eased. Such benefits are not to be taken lightly."[10]

When a disciplined Christian says "I can't afford it," he is referring to more than finances—he knows his spiritual and emotional life can't afford it, either. Nor can his marriage.

Commune Occasion

Use this worksheet to guide you in your money talk. It is based on the suggestions of this chapter.

List of Our Values

His	Hers
_____	_____
_____	_____
_____	_____
_____	_____
_____	_____

How Our Values Relate to Our Spending and Giving

_____	_____
_____	_____
_____	_____
_____	_____
_____	_____

1. How hard are we willing to work for any of the above?
2. How does money and what we can do with it relate to each of our personalities, desires, and dreams?
3. Are we willing to go into debt for the above values? And how do we each feel about debt?
4. Are we both willing to get and use information on budgeting?

ENDNOTES

[1]Ann Rogers, "Hard Times," *Eternity,* April 1980, p. 30. Copyright 1980, Evangelical Ministries, Inc. Used by permission.

[2]Ibid.

[3]Ibid., p. 32.

[4]Charles C. Ryrie, "Owe A Man? OH no, man!" *Moody Monthly,* March 1979, p. 35. Used by permission.

[5]Ibid.

[6]George L. Ford, "Getting Out of the Debt Trap," *Christian Herald,* April 1979, p. 46. Copyright 1979 by Christian Herald. Used by permission.

[7]Ibid., p. 49.

[8]Rogers, "Hard Times," *Eternity*, p. 32.

[9]Ford, "Getting Out of the Debt Trap," *Christian Herald,* p. 47.

[10]Ryrie, "Owe a Man? OH no, man!" *Moody Monthly,* p. 37.

CHAPTER SIXTEEN

WHEN ONE PLUS ONE EQUALS THREE
PONDERING PARENTHOOD

Future shock, according to sociologist Alvin Toffler, is caused by overchoice. Compared to the past we are overcome by being forced to make countless decisions. Push your cart down a supermarket aisle to get Toffler's point. Grandmother had to select from the big four: Wheaties, Corn Flakes, Rice Krispies, Shredded Wheat. Now, it's hard to even locate one of the four among the pictures of monsters, captains, rabbits, and tigers that decorate scores of cereal boxes on the shelf.

But overchoice involves more serious things than what adorns the breakfast table. Having a baby is a major decision today in a way it was not in the past. In recent centuries married couples were just expected to have babies, and it is an obvious fact that they did have children—lots of them. It was the thing to do; and after all, the Psalmist sang of them as *"a gift of the LORD . . . like arrows in the hand of a warrior, so are the children of one's youth. How blessed is the man whose quiver is full of them"* (Psalm 127:3-5, NASB). For them, many arrows made a full quiver; now, just the thought of one makes couples quiver.

A Quiver Need Not Be Full

Society pressures couples to have fewer children. Today it

would be unthinkable to enter marriage aiming to have as many children as possible. People with large families often receive nasty phone calls and hate letters. Nightmarish accounts of overpopulation haunt the wife of childbearing age and her husband.

Family planning does not deny the Psalmist's contention that children are a blessing of the Lord. It is only a matter of how much blessing the modern couple should have. Though we respect the Psalms as God's Word, we also recognize that they were written in the context of an agricultural society. Each new baby was a new farm hand. Children were an economic asset. Today, they are an expensive commodity. Estimates of what it costs to raise a child run a high as $100,000.

Planning to Be Three, Four, or Maybe More

Despite the cost, having children is the normal thing to do for a couple. Less than one out of five of today's couples expect to remain childless. Most couples want to know what the Bible says about planned parenthood, not planned unparenthood.

Actually, neither Catholics nor Protestants resist limiting the size of the family. The deliberate planning of each birth is not the issue; how you carry out the plan is. The official Roman Catholic position opposes artificial means of birth control (pills, condoms, jellies, diaphragms, etc.). They permit preventing conception through natural means, including the rhythm method (determining the time of the month when conception is likely and abstaining from intercourse then), or abstaining from sex altogether.

The biblical arguments for artificial methods are not complicated. First, since there are other purposes for sex than conceiving babies, sex in marriage is in God's will even when conception is prevented. The pleasure and closeness that a man and wife receive through sexual relating is equally important as having children. Catholic theologians insist that procreation is the primary purpose; the others are secondary. Therefore, reproduction is so closely linked to sex that the possibility of pregnancy should never be eliminated unless naturally so. Sex is fine for a wife beyond the age of childbearing or during the time of the menstrual cycle when conception could not take place.

Biblically, however, it is easy to see that God created Eve for Adam as a companion. Part of their unique intimacy is sexual. The experience of sex is as much a fruit of sex as children are. So a couple need not deliberately be open to conception every time they physically unite.

The second biblical pillar of the family planning argument is found in Genesis 1:28: *"God blessed them and said to them, 'Be fruitful and increase in number; fill the earth and subdue it. Rule over the fish of the sea and the birds of the air and over every living creature that moves on the ground.'"* Protestants maintain that mankind is not only ordered to populate the earth but also to control it. Man may use the knowledge gained by his God-given intellectual powers to exercise that responsible control. This includes using man-made devices for preventing conception from taking place. Your doctor can help you choose the most convenient, reliable, and safe method. If you ask, he will probably have a pamphlet describing clearly your options.

To Be Three or Not to Be Three

Scriptural Issues

Christians who are sure it is all right to use artificial methods to plan their families are not always so certain about using them to remain forever childless. Limiting the family size to one child seems quite acceptable. There is a different reaction to having none than there is to having one.

Our sharp reaction to this is probably because the practice is so new. It's hard to get emotionally adjusted to the idea that couples can enjoy the privilege of sex without the responsibility of parenthood.

A couple that is willing to have at least one child demonstrates that they accept the procreative function which God designed. Therefore, one child seems to justify a lifetime of lovemaking. Not giving in to at least one conception takes away the couple's right to sex. We might reason, if you want marriage, you must want children, at least one. Otherwise, don't get married.

But biblically it seems only logical to justify having no children with the same arguments used to justify having only one or a few. The other purposes of sex in marriage permit couples to engage in it without conceiving any children. As long as enough people are populating the earth, some couples should then be free to decide to be childless. Childless marriages are not new. Twenty percent of married couples over forty were childless in 1950. In 1975 only seven percent were.[1] Today the proportion preferring to be permanently childless is still small, yet the percentage has been increasing in recent years.

Practical Matters

Most modern Christian couples will turn to practical matters in deciding whether or not to become parents.

More Blessed to Live Than to Conceive.   Critics of those who voluntarily choose childlessness accuse them of being selfish. Being a parent is linked to unselfishness. Avoiding parenting amounts to avoiding the cost, inconvenience, and hurt of raising children. Better to buy a boat. The wail of an outboard engine beats the cry of a baby. A career is more fulfilling than motherhood.

These accusations seem to be true. Explaining the choice to postpone motherhood, one writer observes: "Women put off pregnancy while they advanced in their careers, saved for a house, earned a doctorate—or reveled in the narcissism of the Me Decade. 'The thing about babies is that you just can't tuck them in your life neatly,' says New York Publicist Eileen Guiliani.' "[2]

Not all of those who choose a childless marriage do so selfishly, any more than those who choose parenthood do so unselfishly. Some are concerned about the population problems. Certainly, some question whether or not they would be fit parents. And there may be those who feel they can serve God better without children.

In fact, choosing to have a child may be a very selfish act. Couples sometimes do so to "save" their marriage. They believe a child will improve a bad relationship—give them a reason to pull together. Usually this is a poor reason. It's unfair to a child to be counted on doing something he/she is not designed to do. It is possible to have or not have children for the wrong reasons. Couples will want to tidy up their reasons before opting for the parent role.

Authors of a book, *The Parent Test,* give four helpful categories for examining your motives about having children.

Egotistic reasons include things like: having a child who will look like me, who will carry on my admirable traits. Or having a child who will be successful, or one that will carry on my name. Others include "to feel the pride of creation," "to keep me young in heart," "to help me feel fulfilled."

Compensatory motives include: to make up for my own unhappy family background, to make up for lack of satisfaction in my job, to make me feel more secure about my masculinity/ femininity. These can be especially dangerous.

Conforming motives are: to be like most people, to please my parents, to forestall social criticism. These are not as dangerous as the above, but they are still poor reasons for becoming parents because the desire is not to have a child but to please someone else.

Affectionate motives are: "to have a real opportunity to make someone happy," "to teach someone about all the beautiful things of life," "to have the satisfaction of giving myself to someone else," "to help someone grow and develop." These are good reasons for wanting to parent a child.[3]

The Blessings of Birth.   Though you'll want to have these "affectionate" reasons, you'll also probably decide to have a baby because of the rewards. The Psalmist sang, *"Behold, children are a gift of the Lord; the fruit of the womb is a reward"* (Psalm 127:3, NASB).

Most of the award is in the experience itself. Parenting is a participating in God's creative work. Women have a natural baby hunger; some of their creative powers are linked to their reproductive systems. *"A woman giving birth to a child has pain because her time has come,"* observed Jesus, *"but when her baby is born she forgets the anguish because of her joy that a child is born into the world"* (John 16:21).

Ninety percent of the motivation is embedded deeply in the hearts of a husband and wife. At the same time, they are compelled to resist this urge. Arguments pile up: too much work, too expensive, the times are too depressing, we just aren't sure if we'll make good parents. The tension over whether to conceive or not to conceive is great. "Why are we amazed that two people in love would seek the fruit of that love, wish to develop it, and be willing to sacrifice tremendously for it?" ask Mark and Anne Hanchett. "Most often we will find that they are simply doing what seems natural in God's plan for His creation."[4]

One career woman expressed it this way: "My mother told me that if people thought everything through, nobody would ever have children. After I had my daughter, I found I *wanted* to have more. I said, wow, what happened to the career woman?"[5]

The very awesome process of pregnancy and birth is an overwhelming experience to participate in. *"You knit me together in my mother's womb. I praise you because I am fearfully and wonderfully made; your works are wonderful, I know that full well"* (Psalm 139:13-14).

Children also afford an opportunity for growth. Though parenting is tough, it also toughens. Recently I heard someone say, "I used to think that adults made children; now I know that children make adults." Our children stretch us. They teach us humility whenever they respond in exactly opposite ways to our efforts to raise them.

The Hanchetts remind us that they bring refreshment. "Many times a weary, even angry, shopper has been drawn out of his despondency after a few moments with a two-year-old who simply smiles at him. What father has not been soothed by his little son's welcome home. What mother is not enchanted by the tiny girl playing peek-a-boo through her miniature fingers."[6]

Don't Move Forward with Blinders. All of the benefits of having the patter of little feet around the house should not blind us to the fact that these pattering feet can mess it up considerably. Hardly any new father or mother is prepared for the demands of parenthood. One authority claims: "Deciding to have a child is still about the most impactful decision a woman makes."[7]

Now some sociologists are even telling us that the long term rewards are not what they used to be. There is little reward for parents after their children are grown. Children don't bring lifetime happiness to couples. The findings of Norval Glenn and Sara McLanahan dispute the idea that the primary rewards for having children come during middle age and later. Older people, the researchers note, get more satisfaction from their friendships with others than they do from their association with their grown children. The grown children even seem to compete or interfere with those friendships.

> Older people who have expected close relationships with their offspring often feel neglected; parents who have expected that in their old age they would receive gratitude

and repayment of various kinds for the sacrifices they have made for their children are very likely to be disappointed. The best evidence now available indicates that present young adults should not decide to have children on the expectation that parenthood will lead to psychological rewards in the later stages of life. The prospects seem rather dim, at best.[8]

Experts, therefore, are cautioning young couples, for whatever reasons you want to have a child, be sure you are willing to bear it. Once you're decided, you'll want to get ready first not for the baby, but for the pregnancy.

Prepped for Pregnancy

Prize or Surprise

Stepping through the front door into a room drenched with music and perfumed air, the husband spies the candlelit dining room and his wife standing beside the formally set table. She throws her arms around him and whispers, "I've been to the doctor's today; we have something to celebrate."

Unfortunately, the announcement of a "blessed event" doesn't always happen that way. When a baby is wanted and expected, the occasion can be terrific. Marvin Inmon recalls how great the experience was for him and his wife.

> After waiting 12 years for our first child, Rita and I had decided that we wanted to share the birth experience as totally as possible. On the day after Easter, 1978, we performed our own early pregnancy test, which takes two hours. After running the test Rita left for work not knowing the results. I probably checked that little vial 10 times during the next two hours. When the small dark ring appeared at the vial's bottom, I was elated and had the pleasure of calling Rita to say, "We're pregnant."[9]

If the conception is not expected—an "accident"—the situation is quite different. Reactions begin with the cessation of the wife's menstrual flow. Being ten days late tells her and her husband that there is a good possibility she is pregnant. Just a few days late is enough to turn on their anxieties. After a week, they give each other assurances of how it just couldn't be. By ten days they are asking questions like, "How can you stop working now?" "I don't think I'm ready to be a father."

Since it takes thirteen days before a test can be given to confirm the pregnancy, you sleep nervously and sometimes lie awake pondering the threatening changes to your life. Something is about to take away your freedom. You are not going to have a baby, you are having a disruption.

Shock may set in when the doctor's report finally confirms your suspicions. You have conceived, as inconceivable as it might be.

Whether the news of pregnancy shocks or raptures you, as a Christian you'll know that having a baby is ultimately the Creator's work, not yours. As you cooperate with Him in this process, He will give you grace during the months of waiting.

Gestation Aggravation

Better be ready for more than just waiting, though. Pregnancy can be a challenging experience. The possible physical discomforts are well known: ankle swelling, sore breasts, nausea, vomiting, fatigue, heartburn, bleeding, bloated. But couples aren't always aware of the emotional stress that you bear while bearing.

Naturally, couples will react differently through pregnancy just as they would react differently going through Disney World. Some reactions are common; just knowing about them will help you face them.

One woman explains her first reaction.

Your notion of bodily integrity is violated in a much more dramatic fashion than the advent of the first menses or the first act of intercourse . . . you are bound to feel at times that your body has been possessed and that you have lost control of your own person. You can view it as a violent siege, an opportunity for physical transcendence, a chance to see if your body functions properly, or a slight inconvenience—well worth the price—but pleasure and pain will always go hand in hand, and ambivalence is the only correct, the only possible emotional posture. Every transition brings its share of fears (ready dangers and specific problems) and anxieties (a diffuse sense of danger, unspecific tension), and they are in abundance when you are having a baby, which calls for a whole new lifestyle.[10]

The physical changes in the body are, in themselves, enough to cause emotional fluctuations and disturbances. Serious questions about the development of the baby may keep the pregnant woman awake at night. While she may be watching her diet and doing all the doctor tells her, she knows she can't control everything related to a child's normal growth. She reads of Down's syndrome and learns about numerous childhood diseases she never heard of before.

Anxiety about her unseen, unknown passenger is quite normal. Being committed to God's will answers these worries, but won't keep them from coming to you. God, in His sovereignty, will have His will; He will not test us beyond what we are able to bear. Even He, somehow, is in control when babies are born with problems. A man was born blind, according to Jesus, not because of any parental wrongdoing, but for the glory of God (John 9:3). Speaking of His control over all things, God said to Moses: *"Who gave man his mouth? Who makes him deaf or dumb? Who gives him sight or makes him blind? Is it not I, the LORD?"* (Exodus 4:11).

Inner anxieties might produce intense and frightening dreams. Women report a common dream of a mother mistreating her baby or not caring for it properly. It will help her if she shares these with her husband. And prayer is a major way to attack worry. *"Do not be anxious about anything,"* said Paul, *"but in everything, by prayer and petition, with thanksgiving, present your requests to God"* (Philippians 4:6). And the peace of God will guard or keep your hearts. The words "will keep your hearts" are the same words that are used for placing a lid on a pot of boiling water. Paul is therefore not promising that the boiling will go away, but God's peace will put a lid on it.

Adjusting Together. The prospective father is in the best place to help. He can reassure his wife that everything is fine whenever doubts fill her vision. He can listen to her expressions of fear and anxiety without scolding her. He knows his calm support will be reassuring to her. But it won't be easy for him to always be sensitive and supporting. The mood swings of his wife may be hard to take. If she seems to be withdrawing from him, this complicates their relationship.

Temporary changes in their relationship might occur. Because she uses up so much emotional energy concentrating on the occupant of her womb, a wife may have little left to console or support her husband. He may feel neglected or unloved. At times he may sense she resents him.

If the wife's rejection is severe and there are other danger signals of a deteriorating relationship, the husband will need to do something about this, discussing it with his wife and even seeing a counselor. However, if the withdrawal is periodic and understandable, he will need to accept it and not react negatively to her.

He will especially help her by enjoying the fun and astonishing aspects of pregnancy. His wife may take delight in the growing fetus, but feel unattractive with her new figure. Avoiding kidding her about her changing size, he can assure her of his own delight in her pregnant look. In fact, he can look forward to the rewards of the fourth month when her slightly fuller figure may make her more appealing than ever.

There is no reason for their sexual relationship to diminish, though bouts of nausea and other physical discomfort may make it less convenient than before. No longer needing to use contraceptives or else having to "work at" getting pregnant, the couple may find sexual intercourse during pregnancy a delightfully new experience. In the final four to six week period, the doctor may advise abstaining. Before that there is no chance of physical harm. During the final months, you can change positions (wife on top or side by side) to make it more comfortable for the wife.

While pregnancy may not cause any physical roadblocks to sexual relations, it may cause some emotional ones. If either partner harbors resentment over the pregnancy itself, it may cause loss of sexual interest.

However, sexual interference usually amounts to lesser matters than the above: emotional changes, fear of harming the baby, and awkwardness. Couples can handle these problems with the same honesty and tenderness they need to bring to their sexual life generally.

The pregnancy months may find the husband wrestling with his own feelings about becoming a father. The intensity of these feelings as well as the emotional frustrations in his wife may actually make him develop physical symptoms of pregnancy. The best thing a prospective father can do is to channel this apprehension about his future into learning about the process of pregnancy and the task of being a father that lies ahead of him.

Practical Considerations. Besides the emotional life of the expectant couple, they will have to grapple with a lot of practical questions: the choice of a gynecologist, the choice of birth situation (home, hospital), whether or not to choose natural birth, arranging for finances.

They will receive a lot of help from the doctor, relatives, and friends. There are excellent pamphlets and books available to help in all of these aspects.

The months may drag along. You can be thankful you're not elephants whose pregnancies last two years.

You'll want to use the months to get ready for what lies ahead. Many childbirth books and classes will prepare you well for the birth. They don't often help you get ready for what happens afterward: being a parent. You'll want to do some thinking and talking about issues related to this task: your feelings about being a parent, your views of discipline, your expectations of each other as father and mother. Remember that unconsciously you will most likely raise your children as you were raised. Looking back on your own childhood will help you understand better how you will behave as a mother or father. Compare these ideas with what you read in books on parenting by Christian authors.

A Final Thought

Birthing a baby together is a very intimate experience, related to your being "one flesh." The couple's unity in love has now actually become physically concrete. I remember an intense feeling of oneness as Ginger and I first looked together at our newborn children, each containing a part of both of us.

Couples who, in the will of God, are unable to bear children still have the joys of marital oneness. Being a parent is the most frightful responsibility a person can have. Realizing that it is handed to you, or not handed to you, by God is what ultimately makes it bearable.

Commune Occasion

Personally ponder your answer to each question and then discuss it with your partner. Proceed one question at a time. It is important that you listen carefully to each other. Identify areas of agreement and disagreement. It may not be comfortable for you to bring these thoughts out into the open. But remember that the disagreements are there whether or not you discuss them. Exposing them to each other will at least give you a chance to work out solutions.

1. What are some reasons you would like to have a child? The following are offered to stimulate your thought. They are not necessarily all valid reasons.

Cooperating with God in procreation
The joy of conceiving and giving birth
Just the thought of being a mother or father
A feeling of obligation
The opportunity to grow personally
The desire to give myself to the development of children
The fulfillment of oneness in our marriage
To make our parents happy
For what it will do for our marriage
Always had the desire to have a family

2. What are some reasons, fears, or anxieties you have about being a father or mother? The following are listed to prompt your thinking, not because they are necessarily right.

Lack of energy to handle responsibilities
Limitation on my freedom
Financial demands
Inability to train and discipline
Change of career or educational plans
Fear about what happens when the child is a teenager
Worry about my dominating the child's life
My personal dislike of children

3. What good feelings and expectations do you have about the experience of pregnancy? (Share from the wife's and

husband's points of view.)

4. What are some anxieties you have about the experience of pregnancy?

5. Do you have a preference for the type of delivery you would like to experience?

6. What strengths do you have that would contribute to your being good parents?

7. How might your own childhood home life influence how you feel about being a parent?

8. In what ways have you been raised by your parents or guardians that might influence how you would raise yours?

9. What are the major responsibilities of a mother? What are those of a father? Do these differ significantly?

ENDNOTES

[1]Judith Blake, "Is Zero Preferred? American Attitudes Toward Childlessness in the 1920s," *Journal of Marriage and the Family* 2 (May 1979): 245, 246. Copyrighted 1979 by the National Council on Family Relations. Reprinted by permission.

[2]Lyn Langway with Diane Weathers, Sharan Walters, Mary Hager, "At Long Last Motherhood," *Newsweek,* March 16, 1981, p. 86. Copyright 1981 by Newsweek Inc. All rights reserved. Reprinted by permission.

[3]William Granzig, Ellen Peck, *The Parent Test,* p. 19, quoted in H. Norman Wright, Marvin N. Inmon, *Preparing for Parenthood* (Ventura, Calif.: Regal Books, 1980), pp. 18, 19.

[4]Mark and Anne Hanchett, "On Having a Family," *The Stony Brook School Bulletin,* February, 1981, p. 1.

[5]Langway, "At Long Last Motherhood," *Newsweek,* p. 86.

[6]Hanchett, "On Having a Family," p. 1.

[7]Robert L. Gould, *Transformations, Growth and Change in Adult Life* (New York: Simon and Schuster, Inc., 1978), p. 97.

[8]Brenda Hirsch, "Parenthood's Dim Rewards," *Psychology Today,* May 1981, pp. 14-15. Reprinted from *Psychology Today* magazine. Copyright 1982 Ziff-Davis Publishing Co. Used by permission.

[9]Wright, Inmon, *Preparing for Parenthood,* p. 94.

[10]Angela Barron McBride, *The Growth and Development of Mothers* (New York: Harper and Row Publishers, Inc., 1974), pp. 30-31.

CONCLUSION

B efore writing this conclusion, I read through each chapter once again to get a feeling for the whole book. One clear impression was this: I've made it too complicated—the countless suggestions for talking, listening, fighting, and even sleeping together. Is marriage that difficult?

Somehow it's hard for us to think of marriage as something difficult to achieve. Some things are supposed to be tough. Becoming a medical doctor is difficult. Being a skilled mathematician takes hard work. Being a professional golfer requires endless hours of practice. But marriage? Surely anyone can pull that off.

Christians may be even more inclined to simplify marriage. We tend to believe that trust in Christ should make the relationship run smoothly. Yet the New Testament never intends that faith should be a substitute for knowledge and hard work. The Apostle Paul said of his ministry: *"I worked harder than all of them."* He quickly added: *"Yet not I, but the grace of God that was with me"* (1 Corinthians 15:10). We are to trust while we work, not trust instead of work.

Something I have been doing while working on the final chapters has helped me deal with this issue of whether marriage is really complicated or whether we just make it that way. I have been reading the best-selling book, *The Complete Book of Running,* by

James Fixx. Imagine someone writing a whole book on running. What could be more simple than running? If you have a fair pair of legs and a decent pair of shoes, you just step outside and do it. And yet, Jim Fixx's book is 314 pages long. In the back, the bibliography lists over 300 articles and books on running. I asked myself, "Just how can anyone make running that complicated?"

I discovered that only the first part of the book is for us every-other-day-run-for-health-and-fun joggers. For us, he answers questions about how far, how fast, in what weather, what to do when dogs attack, etc. The book makes sense. Just a little bit of knowledge can prevent someone from collapsing on the pavement with a busted heart. If the average jogger is going to be prepared for all the circumstances, there is quite a bit to know about running, after all.

Then I learned that the rest of the book is for those who really want to get into running. At this point, the author prompts you to ask, "How good do you want to be?" Then he lists the various classes of runners. Here is the reader's choice: world class; champion class; first class; second class.[1]

Now we are getting to the real reason for such a long book. It takes lots of information to make it to world or champion class.

Maybe the crucial question about marriage is the same question Jim Fixx asks runners to answer: "How good do you want to be?"

What if you both decide to aim for a "world class" marriage? Or at least "champion class"? Then how you listen to each other, how you work out your conflicts, how you fulfill each other sexually, how intimate you become—all these matters take on new meaning.

If you choose to work for "world class," you'll probably not lay this book aside after one reading. You'll come back to it from time to time, rereading a chapter here and a chapter there as you need it. Maybe you'll take time to read together and then discuss what feelings and ideas it stimulates. You'll grapple with the "Commune Occasion" you may have neglected the first time through. And, of course, you'll read other books to develop and enrich your relationship.

Is it fair for me to suggest that all couples aim for "world class?" After all, not many of the millions of us joggers end up at the Boston Marathon.

It is at this point that marriage is different. In marriage, it's dangerous to put forth little effort and aim for less. Having an average marriage is far more difficult than being an average runner. It takes a lot of effort for some people to maintain much of a marriage at all. If we aim for little, we may end up with nothing.

That happens to one-third of the couples in our country who marry. Painful memories and divorce contracts are all that is left of their marriages. Would that many fail if it were so simple?

Perhaps some fail because they thought that it was. They were willing to settle for second or third class, but found that wouldn't work. They tried for little and got less. Is it really fair to yourself and to your spouse to do that? Don't you each deserve a partner who is aiming higher than second class? Wouldn't it be exciting and rewarding if both of you dedicated yourselves to making your marriage "world class"? Why not GO FOR IT!

ENDNOTES

[1] Jim Fixx, *The Complete Book of Running* (New York: Random House, 1977), p. 84.

INTIMATE MARRIAGE:
MORE HELP FOR MAKING IT

Right Before Marriage (Chapters 1, 2):

Miles, Herbert J. *The Dating Game*. Grand Rapids: Zondervan Publishing House, 1975. Though the title mentions a game, this is a serious book. It covers everything from choosing a mate to planning a honeymoon, and does it all from a Christian viewpoint.

Wright, H. Norman. *A Guidebook to Dating and Choosing a Mate*. Irvine, California: Harvest House Publishers, 1978. Like *The Dating Game,* this is a practical book. If it's read along with Miles' book, it will impart a lot of savvy about courtship, true love, and even special problems related to mixing it up before marriage.

Wright, H. Norman, and Roberts, Wes. *Before You Say "I Do."* Irvine, California: Harvest House Publishers, 1978. This is a do-it-yourself book; it contains a guide for studying the major passages of Scripture about marriage. Also, it has exercises and questionnaires to help a couple analyze and discuss their relationship.

Laying the Foundation (Chapters 3, 4, 5):

Brandt, Henry, and Landrum, Phil. *I Want My Marriage to Be Better*. Grand Rapids: Zondervan Publishing House, 1976. Explains how problems arise in marriage; gives biblical answers.

Achieving the Impossible—Intimate Marriage

Clinebell, Charlotte H., and Clinebell, Howard J. *The Intimate Marriage.* New York: Harper & Row, 1970. One of the clearest, most insightful books about intimacy ever written.

McDonald, Gordon. *Magnificent Marriage.* Wheaton, Ill.: Tyndale House, 1976. Readable, biblical, practical guidelines for many facets of marriage.

Oden, Thomas. *Game Free: The Meaning of Intimacy.* New York: Delta, 1974. Profound discussion of intimacy from contemporary point of view.

Peterson, J. Allan; Petersen, Evelyn; and Smith, Joyce. *Two Become One: Bible Studies on Marriage and the Family for Couples and Groups.* Wheaton, Ill.: Tyndale House, 1973. A Bible study guide on the Scriptural foundations of marriage; it provides an excellent introduction to the basic texts.

Communication (Chapter 6):

Miller, Sherod; Nunnally, Elam E.; Wachman, Daniel B. *Alive and Aware.* Minneapolis: Interpersonal Communications Programs, Inc., 1976. A technical but practical book on analyzing how you talk and how you listen in your relationship. Working through this book will reveal any weaknesses you have in communicating.

Powell, John. *The Secret of Staying in Love.* Niles, Ill.: Argus Communications: Grove Books, 1975. Warmly written, brief paperback making you desire in-depth communion. Has exercises used in marriage encounter weekends.

Small, Dwight H. *After You've Said I Do.* Old Tappan, N. J.: Fleming H. Revell, 1968. The single most insightful book on marital communication ever written. Profound.

Tournier, Paul. *To Understand Each Other.* Translated by John S. Bilmour. Atlanta: John Knox Press, 1967. Very personable, easy-to-read book with a depth of understanding about understanding. You'll understand it. You'll like it.

Wright, H. Norman. *Communication: Key to Your Marriage.* Glendale, Calif.: Regal Books, 1974. This should be the first book a couple would buy on communication in marriage. It's brief, but it attacks the major problems.

Sexual Relations (Chapters 7, 8):

Dillow, Joseph C. *Solomon On Sex.* Nashville: Thomas Nelson, 1977. Handles love, sex, and romance by commenting on the Song of Songs. Beautiful and practical.

Eichenlaub, John E. *The Marriage Art.* New York: Dell Publishing Company, 1969. Written especially for the man, it is filled with insights and suggestions for being a thoughtful, artful lover. Has some special, specific instructions for the honeymoon that should get any couple off to a good start.

La Haye, Tim, and La Haye, Beverly. *The Act of Marriage: The Beauty of Sexual Love.* Grand Rapids: Zondervan Publishing House, 1976. This is a "how to" manual, done frankly, but sensitively. Shows how sex can be a total experience as well as a sensual one.

Wheat, Ed, and Wheat, Gaye. *Intended for Pleasure.* Old Tappan, N. J.: Fleming H. Revell, 1977. The single best, most comprehensive sex manual written from a Christian viewpoint. Answers almost any question; gives help with some possible bedroom problems.

Handling Conflict (Chapters 9, 10):

Augsburger, David. *Caring Enough to Confront.* Glendale, Calif.: Regal Books, 1973. Christian author shows how clashes are part of love. Urges couples to face, not avoid, conflict.

Bach, George, *The Intimate Enemy.* New York: William Morrow and Company, 1969. A very comprehensive book on conflict in marriage, written by one of the early starters in the study of the family. Loaded with insights.

Wright, H. Norman. *The Christian's Use of Emotional Power.* Old Tappan, N. J.: Fleming H. Revell, 1974. Especially helpful for suggestions on understanding and handling anger. A short paperback that is long on insight.

Developing Spiritual Oneness (Chapter 12):

Brown, Joan Winmill, and Brown, Bill. *Together Each Day: Daily Devotions for Husbands and Wives.* Old Tappan, N. J.: Fleming H. Revell Co., 1980. Best for its brevity. Daily portions are not too meaty or complex. Thus it is good for the couple who is just starting to meet with God together.

Krutza, Vilma, and Krutza, William. *His/Hers Devotionals.* Grand Rapids: Baker Book House, 1971. Full of bite-size daily portions of biblical thoughts about marriage. Leads a couple to each other, while directing them to God.

Marriage Roles (Chapter 13):

Elliot, Elisabeth. *Let Me Be a Woman.* Wheaton, Ill.: Tyndale, 1976. Written for women, this book takes the view that submission is biblical and practical; the author spells it out in specific ways.

Gundry, Patricia. *Heirs Together: Biblical Equality in Marriage.* Grand Rapids: Zondervan Publishing House, 1978. Builds a case for making marriage a democracy; the author does not see headship and submission in traditional terms.

Knight, George W., III. *The New Testament Teaching of the Role Relationship of Men and Women.* Grand Rapids: Baker Book House, 1977. Scholarly interpretation of the key passages of Scripture dealing with the issue of roles in marriage. Author takes a traditional view, but defends it very well. Handles issues that are not fully answered by those who want to disregard different roles for the husband and wife.

Miles, Herbert J., and Miles, Fern H. *Husband-Wife Equality.* Old Tappan, N. J.: Fleming H. Revell, 1979. One of the first books by a Christian to spell out in practical terms how an equal marriage really works.

Handling Crises (Chapter 14):

Ahlem, Lloyd H. *How to Cope With Crisis and Change.* Glendale, Calif.: Regal Books, 1978. Short treatment of coping, but an excellent introduction to the subject.

Barrett, Roger. *Depression: What It Is and What to Do About It.* Elgin, Ill.: David C. Cook Publishing Co., 1977. A Christian psychologist gives us an easy-to-read analysis of depression and some suggestions for handling it. It is biblical and realistic.

Bayly, Joseph. *The View from a Hearse.* Elgin, Ill.: David C. Cook, 1969. Written by a leading evangelical who himself has lost three sons; full of realistic understanding and biblical hope.

Miller, William A. *When Going to Pieces Holds You Together*. Minneapolis: Augsburg Publishing House, 1976. A nontechnical approach to grief; offers help to the griever and to the one helping the one in sorrow.

Pincus, Lily. *Death and the Family*. New York: Random House, 1976. Thorough discussion of grief and its effects on family members. Insights come from the experiences of the author, a social worker, seventy years of age at the time of the book's writing.

Financial Matters (Chapter 15):

Burkett, Larry, *What Husbands Wish Their Wives Knew about Money*. Wheaton, Ill.: Victor Books, 1977. A thorough guide, based on Christian values; sensible, helpful.

Hurley, Gale. *Personal Money Management*. Englewood Cliffs, N. J.: Prentice-Hall, 1981. For a better marriage, every couple should have one good sex manual and one comprehensive financial book. And both should be read by both, several times. Here is a practical, up-to-date book on the financial side of things that will serve you well.

Preparing to be Parents (Chapter 16):

Dinkmeyer, Don, and McKay, Gary D. *Systematic Training for Effective Parenting*. Circle Pines, Minn.: American Guidance Service, 1976. This book is used as a manual for a national parent training program that is offered in schools, Y.M.C.As, other community centers. Though it doesn't base its principles on Scripture, it still has a lot of effective guidelines for today's parents.

Dobson, James. *Dare to Discipline*. Wheaton, Ill.: Tyndale House, 1970. A psychologist who dares to take a Christian viewpoint. Dobson has spelled out some principles that the parent should not dare to do without.

Wright, H. Norman. *Preparing for Parenthood*. Ventura, Calif.: Regal Books, 1980. This book will answer a lot of questions and raise the necessary issues related to becoming a parent for the first time.

SCRIPTURE INDEX

SUBJECT INDEX